TaRGET
First Certificate

Nick Kenny
and
Roger Johnson

HEINEMANN

Heinemann International
A division of Heinemann Publishers (Oxford) Ltd
Halley Court, Jordan Hill, Oxford OX2 8EJ

OXFORD LONDON EDINBURGH
MADRID ATHENS BOLOGNA PARIS
MELBOURNE SYDNEY AUCKLAND SINGAPORE TOKYO
IBADAN NAIROBI HARARE GABORONE
PORTSMOUTH (NH)

ISBN 0 435 28196 8

First published 1993

ACKNOWLEDGEMENTS

The authors would like to thank all those students and colleagues from the British Council, Milan, the International Language Academy, Cambridge, and The Cambridge Office, who have provided such a source of inspiration over the years.
Special thanks are due to Barbara Lewis, Beth Weighill, and Margaret Twelves, for their help and advice with the manuscript. Our greatest debt, however, is to our excellent editing team, Sue Jones and Xanthe Sturt Taylor, without whose patient support no book would have been possible.

The publishers would like to thank Mark Bartram, Dave Millican, Heather Skea, Ian Swindale, Front. Alpha, Helen Angelopoulos (Front. Angelopoulos), Mr. Athanasopoulos (Front. Athanasopoulos), Mary Kitsou, Front. Konstantos, Maria Patsis (Front. Patsis), Edel Conway Rigas, Front. Theodoropoulu, Mr. Trehas (Front. Trehas) and Mr. Tsiros (Front. Stratigakis)

We would like to thank the following for permission to reproduce copyright material:
Aitken & Stone excerpt from novel '4.50 from Paddington' by Agatha Christie, p59; Joyce Bond for 'Dogsbody' article, p36; Michele Elliot for 'Modern Manners' text, p42; Express Newspapers plc for 'Pack up your Troubles' by Neville Hodgkinson,p85; 'Just Potty about Paddington' by Graham Lord,p136; 'Gory Riddle of Wolfman' by Graham Bell, p54, 'Are you safe to out without a smog mask' by Cathy Scott-Clark,p146; Debrett's and Elsie Burch-Donald for extract from Visitors and Houseguests (Debrett's Etiquette and Modern manners) Pan books, p42;The Flora Project for text from their booklet 'Eating for a Healthy Heart', p88/89; Friends of the Earth for extracts from 'Help Us Stop This Destruction', p152; The Guardian for 'Road to Freedom' by Berry Ritchie from Travel (World Tour) section,p78/79; 'Express Coffee Machine' text and diagram from Education Guardian,p102/103; Here's Health for article 'Easy Ways to Beat a Cold' by Leon Chaitow, p126; Home Office for extracts from 'Practical Ways to Crack Crime' - The Handbook p48/51; IPC magazines for 'Hands down for fingerprinting' in Family Circle magazine, p6/7, and 'Parachuting changed my life' in Living magazine, p167; Moneywise Magazine for 'Trends' article by Debbie Kent, p108; The National Magazine Co for article on 'Foreign Exchange' (House Beautiful), p37; Peters Fraser & Dunlop Group Ltd for extract from 'Long Live the Queen' by Ruth Rendell, p164; Radio Times for 'Fashion's Victim', p68, and 'Play it Safe', p119; Random Century Group and Estate of Barbara Pym for extract from 'No Fond Return of Love' by Barbara Pym, published by Jonathan Cape, p10/11; Redwood Publishing for extract from 'Chocolate tasting is like wine tasting - you don't swallow' interview with Sandy Collyer by Candida Crewe - Marks & Spencer Magazine, p18/19; Sainsbury's for extracts from 'Sainsbury's Living Today' leaflets, p112/166; JW Spear & Sons plc for text on 'Scrabble', p63; Tesco for text from Multisaver leaflet, p132; Mrs Margaret Twelves for 'Scrabble Activity', p63/64.

Illustrations by:
Joyce Bond – Dogsbody advertisement, p36; Nicky Dupays – 'Play it Safe' illustration, p119; Paddington Bear illustration by Peggy Fortnum/HarperCollins Publishers, p137; London Underground Map – LRT Registered User No. 92/1652 – Courtesy of the London Transport Museum, p80; 'A Bear Called Paddington' – Cover illustration by David McKee/HarperCollins Publishers, p136; 'Cold Shower' illustration by Wendy Sinclair/Art Resource, p125; Caroline Jayne Church, p56; Cathryne Fitzpatrick, p42; Hardlines, p6, p34, p68, p80, p83, p110, p118, p150; Tony Maguire, p9, p37, p58, p69, p70, p95; Martin Sanders, p21, p34, p35, p51, p62, p105, p121, p112, p113, p114, p126, p152;
Wendy Sinclair, p35, p57, p124.

Photographs by:
Ace Photo Agency,p33, p148, Action Plus Photographic,p61; All-Sport (UK) Ltd ,p61; Anthony Blake, p87, p91; Camping & Outdoor Centre, Oxford p9; Caterskill Management Ltd, p9; Cephas Picture Library p1,p106,p117; Colorific! p148; Colorsport, p127; The Environmental Picture Library, p153; Express Newspapers plc 'Smog mask' photos, p145/146; Financial Times Picture Library, p175; The Flora Project for Heart Disease Prevention,p88/89; Format Partners Photo Library, p52; Paul Freestone, p4, p9, p19, p20, p24, p41, p59, p63, p88/89, p91, p101, p110, p136; Sally and Richard Greenhill, p101, p127, p134, p135; Robert Harding Picture Library Ltd, p9, p117, p131, p134, p135; The Hutchison Library, p37; The Independent ,p160, p175; The International Stock Exchange Photo Library, p17, p91; The Image Bank, p1, p25, p75, p77, p91, p117, p127, p148; Images Colour Library Ltd, p28, p53, p87; Impact Photos Ltd, p13, p17; Lea & Perrins Ltd, p98; The Maker's Hand, p20; Mary Evans Picture Library, p100; Mc Cann Erickson 'Sunburn' photo, p120; NHPA, p153; Carole Ritchie, p79; Safeway Stores Plc, p132; Tony Stone Worldwide Photolibrary, p17, p28, p37, p148; The Telegraph Colour Library Ltd, p33, p52, p91, p148; Tolana, p106; Tropix Photographic Library, p13, p87; Trutex, p13; Viewfinder Colour Photo Library, p33, p148; Zanussi Limited, p117.

Cassettes produced by James Richardson at Studio AVP

Cover design by Stafford & Stafford
Cover illustration by Iwona Abrams

Designed by Stafford & Stafford

Printed and bound in Spain by Mateu Cromo

93 94 95 96 97 98 10 9 8 7 6 5 4 3 2 1

Dear Student

TARGET FIRST CERTIFICATE has been designed to help you prepare for the First Certificate examination in a number of ways.

Firstly, you will find that a large part of each unit consists of a variety of exercises, all of which develop the important skills necessary to pass the First Certificate examination. You need to revise the main grammar structures, extend your vocabulary, improve your reading and listening comprehension, and develop confidence in listening, speaking and writing.

Secondly, there are 'Help' sections throughout the book giving you advice on how to approach the various question types found in the examination. It is not enough just to practise the exam-type questions, you also need help and guidance on what is expected, and the best way to prepare.

Thirdly, you will find Revision Test sections which consist of the type of questions you have to answer in the examination. These can be found at the end of each unit, and also test how well you have learnt the vocabulary and structures presented in the book so far. Unit 12 contains a complete mock examination, so before you do your exam you will know exactly what to expect.

We hope that you will enjoy using this book and wish you the best of luck in your examination.

Best wishes

Nick Kenny Roger Johnson

CONTENTS

CONTENTS

UNIT 1 FIRST SIGHT

READING

Louisa, Lars and Akemi have each written a short description of themselves as part of a pen-friend scheme organised by their teachers. Read the passages as quickly as possible and decide

1 who drives to work.
2 who has a long summer holiday.
3 who learns English at work.
4 which one would make the most interesting pen friend.

Tell your partner which one you chose and why.

My name's Louisa. I'm 19 years old and come from Bologna in Italy. I'm a student at the university, where I study Law. Most of my lectures are in the afternoon, so I usually get up late and study in the evenings. At weekends, I often go to the cinema with my friends in the winter, or to the seaside in the summer. My family has a house on the Adriatic coast, and we all go there every summer for two months. I'm very interested in environmental issues, and would like to meet students from other countries who share my views.

My name's Lars. I'm 26 years old and I come from Malmo in Sweden. I'm a trainee manager in a company which sells office equipment. I spend one week of each month in a different department so that I learn various aspects of the work. I generally spend at least one day per week out of the office as my job involves sales and marketing. My job's very interesting but rather tiring. I get up early each morning and drive ten miles to my office, but I still find the time to study English, because a teacher comes to the company twice a week. In my spare time I like to go skiing and I enjoy all water sports.

My name's Akemi. I'm 25 years old and I come from Tokyo in Japan. At the moment I'm living in Cambridge, where I'm a student of English at a language school. My interests are theatre, cinema and classical music, especially opera. In Japan I work in a large department store selling cosmetics. When I go home I hope to get a job using my English, maybe in a travel agency. My ambition is to travel all over Europe and learn another European language.

5 Now complete this table for each of them, yourself and for your partner.

	Louisa	Lars	Akemi	You	Your partner
Age					
Nationality					
Occupation					
Interests					

6 What questions did you ask your partner to get the information?

How ____________________? Where ____________________?

What ____________________? What ____________________?

Which grammatical tense did you use? Why?

7 Now ask the questions to as many people as possible in your group, and make a note of their replies. Compare with your partner.

8 Write a short passage about yourself for inclusion in the pen-friend scheme.

GR p177

GRAMMAR
Present Simple

1 Study these examples of the use of the Present Simple tense. Notice the two columns on the right which tell you the grammatical tense used in the phrase and the time which is being referred to.

The **Present Simple** tense is used to talk about:

	Tense	Time
States		
He is tall and thin	Present Simple	Always
He isn't American	Present Simple	Always
Habits and routines		
She gets up early	Present Simple	Usually
She wears casual clothes	Present Simple	Usually
She doesn't eat lunch at home	Present Simple	Usually
Things which are always true		
Britain has a temperate climate	Present Simple	Always
Cotton doesn't grow in Britain	Present Simple	Always

Now compare this with the **Present Continuous** tense, used to talk about what is happening now.

	Tense	Time
She wears expensive clothes	Present Simple	Usually
She's wearing jeans	Present Continuous	Now
The sun rises in the east	Present Simple	Always
The sun is rising	Present Continuous	Now

2 Put a verb in these sentences in the correct tense.

1 Roland usually ________ a raincoat, but today he ________ an anorak instead.
2 Linda ________ at 8.00 a.m. every day and ________to work by car.
3 Frances never ________ high-heeled shoes, in fact she usually ________ sandals.
4 Matthew ________ in the centre of town but this week he ________ at his parents' house in the country.
5 Alex is a very reliable person, everybody ________ him.

VOCABULARY

Clothes

1 Look around the room and make a list of all the articles of clothing that you can see.
2 Compare lists with a partner.
3 Add to the list some articles of clothing that you cannot see, but which people sometimes wear (maybe at another time of year).
4 Divide your list into 4 groups of words. You can decide how to divide them, but each group must have a title.
5 Show your groups to your partner and explain why you have grouped the articles in this way.
6 Look at these words. What type of words are they?

long	cotton	plain	thick	striped
high-heeled	leather	thin	woollen	short
long-sleeved	waterproof	light	checked	heavy
short-sleeved	flat-heeled	silk	loose-fitting	tight-fitting

7 Which of these words can be used to describe which clothes? Choose one article of clothing from your list to put after each adjective.

Order of Adjectives

1 Look at these phrases:

a full-length red overcoat
a pair of red and white striped cotton socks
a loose-fitting black woollen pullover
a pair of brown leather shoes
a short-sleeved green cotton sweatshirt
a pair of white flat-heeled sandals
a plain blue cotton T-shirt

Now make similar phrases to describe articles of clothing that you can see.

2 What do you notice about the order of the adjectives?

3 Look at the four pictures below. Write one sentence describing the clothes worn by the person in each picture.

4 Link each of the expressions in the box to one of the pictures.

5 Write two more phrases to describe the people in the photographs.

a	in her early thirties
b	in his late teens
c	with short blond hair
d	with dark curly hair
e	with short dark hair
f	slim
g	of average height and build
h	well-dressed
i	casually-dressed
j	heavily made-up

1

3

2

4

LISTENING 1

1 Listen to the description of a woman the police would like to interview after a robbery. Is it one of the women in the pictures or not?
Give your reasons.

2 Read this description of a woman the police would like to interview. Listen again and decide if it describes the same woman. Underline any parts which are different.

The woman is tall with short brown curly hair and brown eyes. She was wearing a long grey woollen overcoat and flat shoes, and was carrying a beige leather shoulder bag and an umbrella. She was described as being in her early thirties, and speaking with a Liverpool accent.

3 Write a similar description of another of the people in the photographs – or of one of your classmates.

4 Read your description to your partner or classmates. Can they identify the person?

VOCABULARY

1 Look at these examples.

How does he dress?
What sort of clothes does she usually wear?
What was he wearing yesterday?
She usually wears a skirt and jumper.
She usually wears a dress.
Was she dressed in a skirt or trousers?

1 What is the difference between *clothes* and *dresses*?

2 What is the difference between *to wear* and *to dress*?

2 Using one word only, put the correct form of either *wear* or *dress* in each of the spaces.

1 He is ________ a blue jacket.
2 She was ________ a light summer dress.
3 He always ________ very well on these occasions.
4 This coat is very ________. I need a new one.
5 That ________ is too short for her.
6 He got up, ________ and went to work.
7 She always ________ her son in blue.
8 I don't like that ________ you're ________.

3 1 Look at these words which are used to describe a person's character and decide whether they are positive or negative.

sensible	dull	reliable
amusing	stupid	cold
boring	trustworthy	practical
strong	charming	helpful
selfish	foolish	observant
intelligent	bossy	lively
silly	responsible	fussy
patient	sensitive	friendly
entertaining	careful	honest
nasty	lazy	independent

2 Which of them would you use to describe yourself?

3 Can you add some more adjectives to describe your character?

4 Which words can be made into the opposite by adding a prefix?

Examples: reliable – **un**reliable
patient – **im**patient

5 What are the opposites of the other words?

READING

1 Try to answer these questions with a partner.

1 Why are fingerprints important to the police?

2 How can you take your fingerprints?

First, ______________________________

Then, ______________________________

Finally, ______________________________

3 Now read the text quickly to check your answers. Why are fingerprints important to hand analysts?

4 Now read more carefully and match the words from the text on the left (line numbers in brackets) with the meanings on the right.

whodunnits (1)	of which there is only one
convicted (2)	parts of circles in fingerprints
unwary (2)	proved to be guilty
whorls (4)	murder stories
swirls (4)	careless
unique (5)	complete circles in fingerprints
irrefutable (6)	that cannot be doubted
ascribe (7)	work out the meaning
decipher (9)	link to
smudging (13)	making unclear

FINGER PRINTING

Hands down for clues to your personality

You don't need to be a follower of whodunnits to know that a careless fingerprint has convicted many an unwary villain. But fingerprints can also tell the interested observer a great deal about your personality. Hand analyst Lori Reid explains how to take your own fingerprints – and what the whorls and swirls reveal.

FINGERPRINTS are unique: no two people, not even identical twins, possess the same pattern. They are our very own personal signatures, our calling cards, irrefutable marks of our identity. However, hand analysts have been able to ascribe particular characteristics to the six basic types of pattern of fingerprints.

FINGER patterns are hard to decipher just by looking, but taking a print of them is easy and makes the patterns stand out clearly. Either use the traditional ink pad, or try lipstick or shoe polish. Press the fingertip onto the pad, or rub lightly with lipstick or polish, then press firmly onto a sheet of paper, rolling the fingertip from one side to the other to prevent smudging.

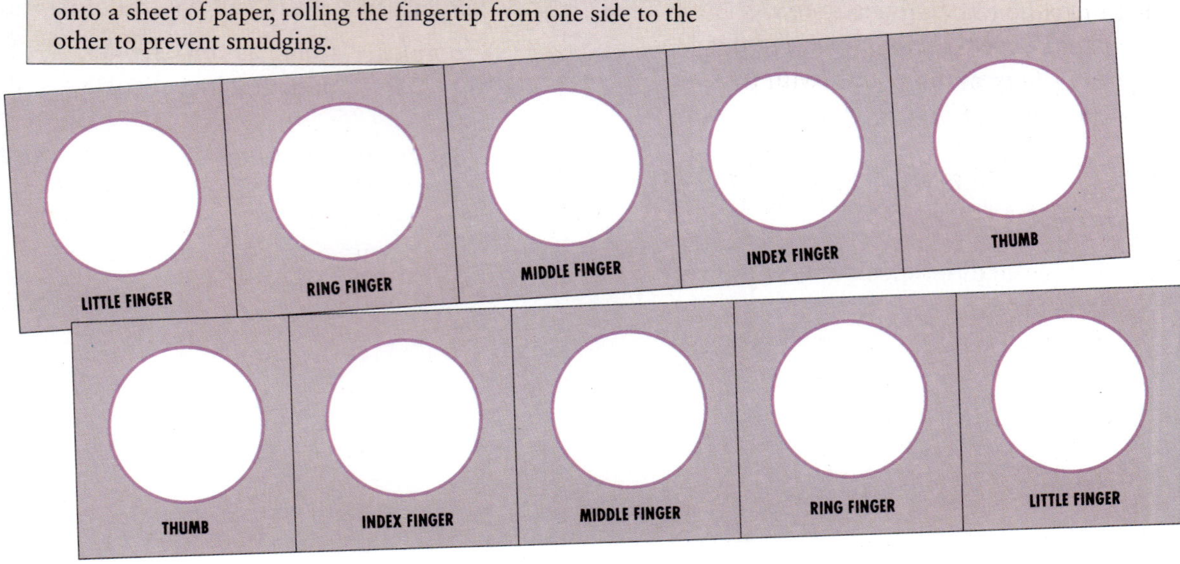

2 Decide who is student A and who is student B. Read your part of the text and answer the questions below.

STUDENT A

THE WHORL

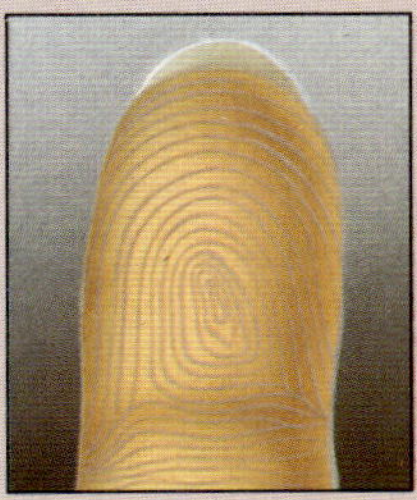

The whorl is the most individual of all the patterns. It denotes a fixed, rather inflexible attitude. Whorl owners hate anyone telling them what to do. On the ring finger it shows an artistic eye and creative appreciation. On the little finger it denotes quiet, deep thinkers.

People with a majority of whorls tend to be slow to respond, and find it difficult to change their views and opinions. This is because 'whorled' types need time to process information; they need to think over and consider their answers.

THE COMPOSITE

This shows an ability to appreciate all points of view and in any occupation where it is necessary to understand a situation from all its angles – a judge, lawyer, or teacher, for example – this pattern is an advantage.

But when it comes to personal decision-making, the composite can be a definite drawback. Because people with this pattern spend so long considering the alternatives, weighing up the pros and cons, analysing their problems from every aspect, they tend to complicate the matter and end up totally confused, unsure which way to turn or which road to take.

STUDENT B

THE ARCH

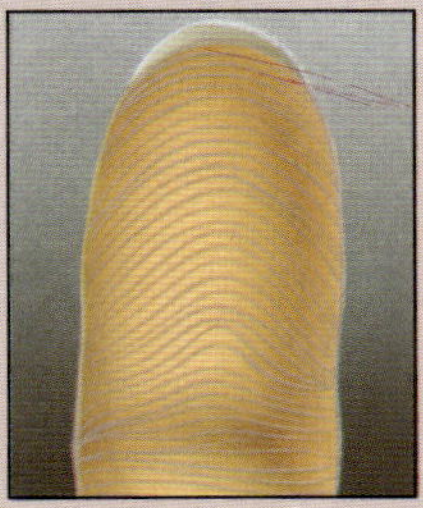

Arches denote a practical, sensible attitude to life. People with this pattern are always ready to help others. Firm realists, their conversation is usually based on everyday subjects or concrete, material topics. They have plenty of common sense, are thoroughly trustworthy and reliable and as such tend to attract people with problems who find them excellent 'shoulders to cry on'. But when it comes to their own problems, they find it very difficult to put their deeper feelings into words and are often in danger of repressing their emotions.

THE LOOP

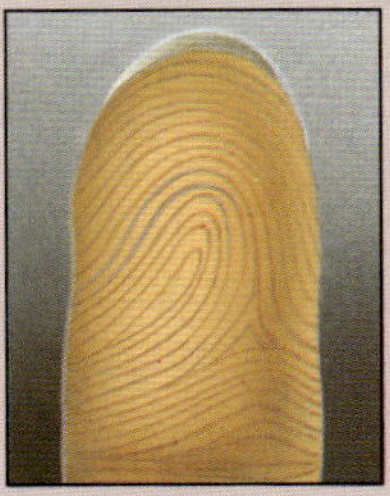

Loops represent flexible, adaptable and versatile individuals. Loop owners are open-minded and tolerant in character and they need a large variety of interests to keep them excited and stimulated throughout their everyday lives. They need a constant change of activities and they thrive on new challenges and opportunities.

Loop owners make excellent communicators and are at their best when they're working or dealing with other people. Any environment where there is a free exchange of news, views and ideas, suits them best. The loop is the mark of creativity. It indicates an open, amenable approach and, above all, a love of new ideas.

1 Underline the words (adjectives and nouns) in the text which best describe the personality of the people with these fingerprints.

2 What other adjectives could you use to describe such people? Choose from those in the box.

unemotional	realistic	helpful
independent	reserved	religious
communicative	thoughtful	creative
sociable	understanding	analytical
lucky	indecisive	adventurous
enthusiastic	imaginative	idealistic
lazy	fair	

3 Is it important which finger the patterns are on?

4 Now tell your partners what you have found out about fingerprints.

5 Look at (or print!) your own fingerprints. Decide which patterns you have, and discuss with your partners whether the descriptions are true for you.

LISTENING 2

You will hear someone giving a talk to a group of students about what to take with them on a walking holiday. Listen and complete these notes, made by one of the students, by putting a word or phrase in each of the numbered blanks.

Travelling to (1) __________ by overnight sleeper train and then getting around by (2) __________. Staying in hostels.

Things to take:

large rucksack	for clothes etc	put name and address
(3) __________	for packed lunch, study materials	put name and address
a full-length, waterproof (4) __________	with a (5) __________	for cold and wet weather
plenty of pairs of (6) __________	cold, wet feet!	
good thick (7) __________	very cold!	
gloves	for long walks	(8) __________ gloves best
strong walking (9) __________	for rough country	(10) __________ ones best
casual shoes	for (11) __________	
small (12) __________	for accidents, etc.	put in some glucose tablets or (13) __________

GRAMMAR GR p177

In Case

1 Look at this phrase from the listening text.

Put your name and address inside and outside each piece of luggage in case it gets lost.

1. What time is referred to? Which verb forms are used?
2. Compare these two sentences. What is the difference in meaning?

   Take a big anorak ***in case*** *the weather is bad.*
   Take a big anorak ***if*** *the weather is bad.*
3. Listen again and make a note of three phrases which include *in case*. Which tense follows *in case* in each example?

2 Complete each of the following sentences in such a way that it means exactly the same as the sentence printed before it.

1. You should take a torch because the car might break down at night.

   In case ______________________________
2. Take an umbrella because it might rain.

   In case ______________________________
3. You should take a large bag because you might decide to do some shopping.

   In case ______________________________
4. Put some plasters in your bag because you might cut yourself.

   In case ______________________________

3 You are going on a day's walk across some rough hill country in Scotland in March. You are properly dressed for the trip and have a packed lunch.

1 Match the articles with the names in the box.

2 You can only carry six of these articles with you. Decide which six are the most important to take and why. Discuss your choice with a partner.

some rope	a water bottle
a box of matches	a tent
a first-aid kit	an umbrella
a sleeping bag	a penknife
a whistle	a rucksack
some chocolate	a map
an extra pullover	an extra pair of socks

3 Write six sentences using *in case* to justify your choice.

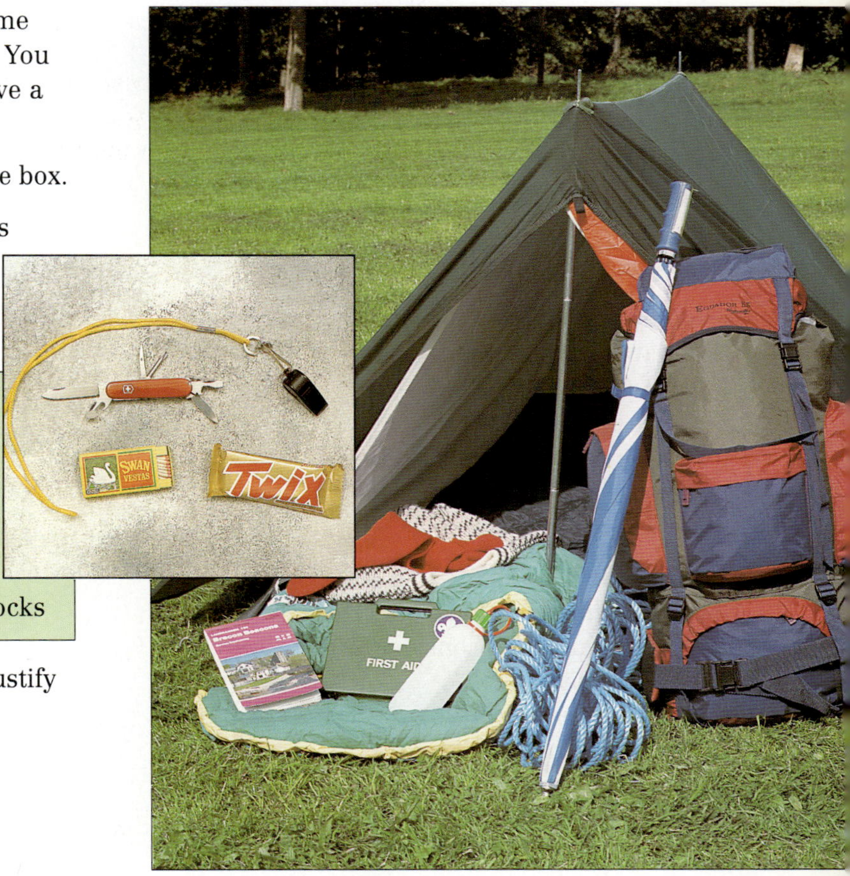

READING

1 Look at the picture. How many things can you name?

This is a short extract from a novel called *No Fond Return Of Love* by Barbara Pym. The style and vocabulary are quite difficult, so don't worry if you can't understand every word. The questions will make the passage easier to understand.

2 Read quickly to answer these questions.

1 Where are the two women?
2 What is their relationship?
3 Where are they going?

3 Read more carefully and find words in the text that have these definitions (the line numbers are in brackets).

1 think about a lot (10)
2 strong heavy cotton cloth (16)
3 allow yourself to consider (20)
4 waiting secretly (21)
5 serious and stern (25)
6 with permanent folds (26)
7 matching pullover and cardigan (27)
8 put into a suitcase (28)
9 being careful with money (35)
10 with lots of air currents (58)

4 Choose the best alternative to define the words from the passage.

1 *fetch* (13) means to go and
a make
b find
c get

2 *eager* (22) means
a ready
b dangerous
c unwilling

3 *snatch* (22) means to take
a silently
b quickly
c secretly

4 *if her glance should stray* (22) means
a if she looked away
b if she fell asleep
c if she got bored

Chapter Twenty

Mrs Williton and Marjorie, as was their invariable custom when travelling, had arrived at Paddington an hour too early for the train. There was therefore nothing to do but to go and have a cup of tea. They had brought their own with them to have on the train, though Marjorie would have liked to have tea in the restaurant car, where there was always the possibility of a romantic or interesting encounter. After all – though this was hardly the time to dwell on it – had she not met Aylwin in very similar circumstances?

'I'll keep an eye on the luggage, dear, while you fetch the tea,' said Mrs Williton, who had found two places at a table. While Marjorie queued at the counter, her mother's eyes never left the two small suitcases and the canvas shopping-bag that they had brought with them. She did not realize that the other travellers were much too preoccupied with their own luggage to entertain any idea of stealing hers. She always imagined that some lurking stranger was lying in wait, eager to snatch away the cases if her glance should stray from them for a moment. But he'd probably be disappointed in what he found, she thought with grim satisfaction, remembering the woollen dresses, grey pleated skirts, hand-knitted twin-sets, and blouses (in case the weather got warmer), which they had packed.

When the train came in they went to their reserved seats,which were in a carriage not too near the engine (in case there should be an accident) and, of course, in the second class.

Aylwin had always tried to persuade Marjorie to travel first class, but Mrs Williton's natural thriftiness would not hear of this. Money could be put to better uses — the organ fund, for example. Again, Marjorie would have liked to travel first class. The possibilities of a romantic encounter were as great in a first class carriage as in the dining car – greater, even. One never met anybody interesting travelling second class. Their seats offered some advantage, however – to Mrs Williton if not to Marjorie. They were on the corridor side, so that Mrs Williton could slip easily and comparatively unnoticeably to the lavatory. This meant, however, that she would not have control of the window, but, as she whispered to Marjorie, 'You can't have everything.'

As they entered the carriage, a silent middle-aged couple were already preparing to occupy the window seats, and the man was in the act of getting up and shutting the window. This was very disquieting, and Mrs Williton foresaw a tense atmosphere all the journey. She would be worrying about whether she was getting enough air, and then, if she did pluck up her courage and ask for the window to be opened, it might become too draughty. She sat down stiffly on the edge of the seat, like a bird on an unfamiliar nest.

Marjorie opened her favourite woman's magazine and turned to the serial, hoping to lose herself in it.

5 *slip* (44) means to leave
- a quietly
- b quickly
- c normally

6 *disquieting* (53) means
- a worrying
- b annoying
- c comforting

7 *foresaw* (53) means
- a feared
- b hoped for
- c predicted

8 *stiffly* (58) means
- a comfortably
- b tense
- c relaxed

5

1 What type of woman is Mrs Williton? List five things in the text that tell us about her character.

2 What type of woman is Marjorie? Is she like Mrs Williton? List three things in the text that tell us about her character.

3 Who do you think Aylwin is?

4 How does each woman feel at the end of the passage? Why?

6

Write questions about Mrs Williton and Marjorie to which sentences 1–6 could be the answer.

1 ______________________________?

In case someone tried to steal them.

2 ______________________________?

In case all the seats were taken.

3 ______________________________?

In case the weather got warmer.

4 ______________________________?

In case there should be an accident.

5 ______________________________?

In case she needed to go the lavatory.

6 ______________________________?

In case there was not enough air.

HELP WITH VOCABULARY

Word Building

Here are some examples of the most common types of question found in word-building exercises in the Use of English section.

1 Inserting words describing the same types of things (e.g. clothes).
Put one word in each of the spaces.

Example: In cold weather she often wears a long woollen *scarf* round her neck.

1 People who go jogging usually wear a ________ and trainers.

2 A pair of ________ will keep your hands warm in cold weather.

3 You can buy jeans with either buttons or ________ at the front.

4 In hot weather peopl instead of long trouse

5 When I get home I al shoes and put on a pa ________.

2 Using the same word in forms.
Put the correct form of th of the spaces.

Example: I like *to wear* *Wearing* jean

1 Angelo ________ jeans week.

2 Brenda ________ a red dress and high heels when I saw her.

3 I have only ________ those trousers twice.

4 My old coat is completely ________ out.

5 The shoes were already showing signs of ________.

3 Adding a prefix or a suffix to change the meaning of a word.

Change the word on the right so that it fits into the sentence.

Examples: It's a dangerous game so you must be *careful*. CARE

Everyone likes him because he is so *friendly*. FRIEND

1 He makes people smile because he's so ________. CHEER

2 You can rely on his judgement, he's very ________. SENSE

3 She was never late, I was impressed by her ________. PUNCTUAL

4 I wonder if you could help me, I need some ________. INFORM

h great style and her ıys ________. FASHION

for groups of objects.

ch of the spaces.

were tables, chairs and ther pieces of *furniture*.

lass there are Italians, and many other *lities*.

k, mascara and other _.

ndbag she has two large ________ to carry.

3 Coats, pullovers and jackets are all articles of ________.

4 Students will be provided with breakfast but no other ________.

5 The thieves stole earrings, watches and many other types of ________.

WRITING

Writing your Composition: Presenting a balanced argument

1 Look at these pictures. Describe the clothes that the students are wearing. Why are they wearing these clothes?

2 In Britain it is quite common for school students to have to wear school uniform. Discuss the following with your partner:

1 Do you like the uniforms in the picture?
2 Are uniforms worn in your country? Do you like them?
3 What do you imagine British students think of their uniforms?
4 What are the advantages of wearing a school uniform?
5 Are there any disadvantages?

3 Five school students were asked for their opinions about uniforms. Listen and note down some of the advantages and disadvantages they mention.

Are their opinions the same or different from those you discussed with your partner?

The students were then asked to write a composition about the advantages and disadvantages of school uniforms. Here is the best one for you to read. As you read, think about why it is a good composition, and answer the questions which follow.

What are the arguments for and against compulsory school uniforms?

In many secondary schools in Britian the wearing of a school uniform is compulsory. Some schools argue that there are many advantages to this system, *but* students can often see some disadvantages too.

The main advantage of school uniforms is that they give a common identity to the school. Even when the students are on their way home, everyone knows which school they go to. This is important if the students misbehave, for example. *Another advantage* is that if all the students in a school wear the same type of clothes in matching colours and styles, then they tend to look smart when they are all together. *Finally*, students whose parents can't afford nice clothes look the same as everyone else and so don't feel inferior.

Most students don't agree with school uniforms, *however*, for a number of reasons. *Firstly*, when you have to wear the same clothes as everyone else you don't have a chance to develop personal taste in the way you dress. *Moreover*, people who look scruffy usually look scruffy in their uniforms too and you can always tell the people who come from poor homes because their uniforms are not as new or don't fit properly. *Lastly*, the main reason why most students don't like school uniforms is because most schools choose such horrible colours and styles, that don't suit young people at all.

It is clear, *therefore*, that there are arguments in favour of school uniforms and arguments against. *On balance*, most schools want them, but most students do not.

4 Match the words from the text on the left with the definitions on the right.

smart (para 2)	of the correct size
scruffy (3)	in the same colour or style
match (2)	of an untidy appearance
fit (3)	of the right colour or style for someone
suit (3)	tidy and attractive

HELP WITH WRITING

Paragraphing

1 The composition is divided into 4 paragraphs.

1 How do we recognise a paragraph?
2 How did the writer know when to end one paragraph and begin another?
3 Give each paragraph a title.

2 In the second and third paragraphs, a number of points are made. Here is part of the plan for the composition.

Paragraph 1:	**Introduction**
Paragraph 2:	**Points in favour** a common identity b c
Paragraph 3:	**Points against** a no individuality b c
Paragraph 4:	**Conclusion**

1 Complete the plan by looking back at the composition.
2 Look carefully at the introduction. What information does it contain?
3 Look carefully at the conclusion. What information does it contain?
4 Look carefully at the question. Does it ask for the writer's opinion?
5 What is the writer's opinion? When is it given? Why?

Many of the compositions in the First Certificate exam ask you to discuss a topic like the one in the example. One way of doing this is to present a balanced argument, as this author did, by dividing points for and against into two paragraphs.

3 Look at the words which are in italics. What contribution do they make to the composition? Here are some other ways the writer could have made the same points:

1 *but* students can often see some disadvantages too.
On the other hand, students can often see some disadvantages.
2 *The main advantage* of school uniform is ...
One advantage of school uniform is ...
The first advantage of school uniform is ...
One point in favour of school uniform is ...
The greatest advantage of school uniform is ...
3 *Another advantage* is ...
A further advantage is ...
One other advantage is ...
4 *Finally*,
Lastly,
5 Most students don't agree, *however*,
Most students, however, don't agree.
Most students, on the other hand, disagree.
6 *Moreover*, people who look scruffy ...
What's more, people who look scruffy ...
Secondly, people who look scruffy ...
7 *On balance*, most schools like them ...
To sum up, most schools like them ...
In conclusion, most schools like them ...

Planning

1 To write a good composition you need to think of three separate things:

1. **The subject matter** – what you want to say.
2. **The layout** – how this will be ordered and divided into paragraphs.
3. **The language** – finding the words in English to express what you want to say.

It is very difficult to do all three of these things at the same time. So it is important to think about your composition before you begin. You should decide what you want to say and plan the paragraphs before you begin to write. Then when you are writing you can concentrate on finding the right words and grammatical forms to express your ideas.

The following exercise will help you practise these skills.

2 With your partner or group choose one of these titles for your composition.

1. What can be said for and against a period of compulsory military service for young people?
2. Should sport be part of the school curriculum, or should it be left to the individual to organise?
3. What are the advantages and disadvantages of giving pets as presents?

3 Now talk to your partner and list as many points as you can think of about the argument.

1. Divide the points into advantages and disadvantages.
2. Compare your list with the list of another pair or group who chose the same question. Add any new ideas to your list.
3. Now select the most important points – the ones you want to include in your composition.
4. Think about your composition plan – it will look like this:

Paragraph 1:	**Introductory sentence.**
Paragraph 2:	**Points in favour** (advantages) a b c
Paragraph 3:	**Points against** (disadvantages) a b c
Paragraph 4:	**Conclusion**

Look again at the example composition.

Read the introduction. Now write a similar introduction to your composition, and plan the paragraphs.

4 You are now ready to write the paragraphs of your composition. Remember to use the expressions in italics above.

REVISION TEST 1

1 For each question 1 to 10 you must choose the word or phrase that best completes the sentence.

1 It was clear that the young man was _______ of taking over.
A responsible B reliable C capable D able

2 Your youngest son is remarkably tall _______ his age.
A to B for C by D at

3 She is a tall _______ blonde woman in her early twenties.
A blue-eyes B blue-eyed C blue-eye D blue-eye's

4 An anorak is necessary in case the weather _______ bad.
A be B is C was D will be

5 When appearing in public, the Queen generally _______ formally.
A wears B clothes C dresses D puts on

6 She doesn't take much care of her clothes and so always looks _______.
A scruffy B grumpy C stylish D smart

7 To sum up, _______ , I'd like to thank you all.
A but B therefore C further D while

8 The green overcoat _______ her green woollen dress.
A suited B fitted C copied D matched

9 That coat is too small, you can see it doesn't _______ .
A fit B match C suit D size

10 Take an umbrella in case it _______ .
A rained B will rain C rains D would rain

2 Choose from these compositions:

1 What are the arguments for and against allowing children to choose their own clothes?

2 What are the advantages and disadvantages of living in a place which attracts a lot of tourists?

3 Complete each of the following sentences with one word to form an expression with BY.

Example: All these lovely pullovers are made by *hand* in local homes.

1 This is by _______ the best Indian restaurant in town.
2 Excuse me, I think you've picked up my book by _______ .
3 There was no one to go with me, so I went by _______ .
4 Andy knows all the words to that song by _______ .
5 I've never spoken to her, but I know her by _______ .

UNIT 2 NICE WORK

SPEAKING

Look at the three photographs.

1 Decide:
Which would be the best place to work and why.
Which would be the worst place to work and why.
2 Choose one of the places. Make a list of all the different jobs people do there.
3 Find someone who has chosen the same picture and compare your list. Add any new ideas.
4 Is there a job that you would be good at?

VOCABULARY

1 Look at the list of skills and qualities in the box.

Which of them are necessary for the jobs on your list?
Discuss this with your partner as in the example.

Example: To be a ________ you need to have good ________ skills and to be ________.

Skills	Qualities
computer skills	patient
typing skills	physically strong
driving skills	emotionally strong
telephone skills	well-organised
interpersonal skills	intelligent
artistic skills	caring
language skills	calm
mathematical skills	quick-thinking
managerial skills	honest
financial skills	clean and tidy
	punctual

2 Can you think of some more skills and qualities needed for the jobs on your list?

READING

1 Read this paragraph and decide which job is being described.

To be a _______ you need to have a good general education and good interpersonal skills. You do not need a degree, but you have to do a special training course. Driving skills may be useful and you have to be honest, clean and tidy and very patient. A _______ needs to be calm in a crisis, quick thinking and has to be emotionally strong. They are usually tall, well-built and physically strong but they need to be caring people too.

2 Now choose one of the jobs on your list and write a paragraph about it like the one above.

SPEAKING

Discuss these questions:

1 The food industry is very large. If somebody wanted to make a career in this industry what types of jobs could they train for?

2 Which is more interesting to work in: a restaurant, a supermarket, or a food factory?

3 Make a list of the advantages and the disadvantages of working with food.

READING

1 Read the article quickly to find the answers to these questions:

1 Which company does Sandy work for?
2 What is her job called?
3 What does she have to do?
4 How long has she been in the food industry?

'Chocolate tasting is like wine tasting – you don't swallow'

SANDY COLLYER

Would working as a Confectionery Selector for Marks & Spencer be a dream come true for chocoholics? Candida Crewe finds out.

ONE DAY SANDY Collyer and a colleague of hers had to eat their way through more than 22lbs* of chocolates. It took them from 9am to 2pm. Afterwards they felt 'very, very unwell'. But their chocolate marathon was not a binge. It was all in the course of duty. Sandy is one of the 11 people at Marks & Spencer who are responsible for chocolates and sweets. Her official title is Confectionery Selector. She has to sample chocolates every day.

'That 22lbs was unusual,' she said. 'The technologist and I had to try out an entire fresh cream range from one of our suppliers before it went off. It was a very hot day which made things worse.'
Despite such excesses, Sandy is not overweight. How come? 'Chocolate tasting is like wine tasting,' she told me, 'you don't swallow unless it's so good you can't resist. I think all of us in the office have become immune to chocolate. It no longer makes us put on weight.' Perhaps, after 15 years in the business, Sandy has become immune to the tempations which in her airy offices in the M&S headquarters in Baker Street I found overwhelming. There were chocolates everywhere.

Her chocolate enthusiasms began early. 'When I was little I, like every kid, wanted to work in the Mars Bar factory. When I began in confectionery I was just like a child in a sweet shop, eating everything. But that's worn off. I like chocolate, but I'm not a chocoholic.'

*9.98 kg

2 Now read more carefully and find words which mean:

1 having too much of a good thing (line 5)
2 to try (line 9)
3 complete (line 11)
4 trying food (line 15)
5 well ventilated (line 21)
6 too much (line 22)

3 Are the following statements true or false?

1 Sandy samples 22lbs of chocolates every day.
2 She does not usually eat the chocolates she tastes.
3 She is the only chocolate taster at M & S.
4 She has not put on weight because of her job.
5 She has always wanted to work with food.

4 What qualifications and training do you think Sandy needed to become a Confectionery Selector?

Read about Sandy's career and fill in the chart:

Sandy was brought up in Essex. After A-levels she worked in banking for a year and hated it. Then, encouraged by a friend in retailing, she went to work at Harrods. 'I did my training there. I was a buyer for eight years – bread, patisserie, cakes – before moving into confectionery where I found my niche.'

She enjoyed the challenge, the fast turn-over. In 1987 she moved to Marks & Spencer. Her basic responsibility is to develop new lines and she is in charge of both product and packaging. This involves a lot of travel in Britain and on the Continent, overseeing production, doing comparative shopping and visiting food fairs.

Sandy Collyer

Qualifications:
____
____

Work experience:
______________________ (1 year)
______________________ (8 years)
______________________ (since 1987)

Training:
____

Present responsibilities:
____
(product and packaging)
____
____

GRAMMAR GR p177
to be used to + ing

1 Look at these sentences about Sandy. What is the difference in meaning between a and b?

1 a She eats chocolate every day.
  b She's used to eating chocolate every day.
2 a In her job she travels a lot.
  b She's used to travelling a lot in her job.

When do we use the form *to be used to* +ing?

2 Look at these comments made by foreign students living in Britain and answer the questions.

1 When I first arrived I didn't like the food, but now I'm used to eating potatoes every day and I quite like it.

What has changed for Dimitra? Why?

2 I'd studied the grammar, but I wasn't used to speaking and listening. At the beginning, you can't understand anything because it's all so strange, and then gradually you get used to hearing the language, and you begin to understand more.

What changed for Kunio?

3 A friend of mine couldn't stand the weather. She was here for four weeks, but never got used to feeling so cold and went back as soon as possible. I felt cold at first, but I'm used to it now and so I don't really notice.

Why was Ronaldo's friend unhappy? What didn't change for her? What changed for Ronaldo?

You are used to **verb +ing**
You get used to **verb +ing**
You are used to (the) **noun**
You get used to (the) **noun**

3 Use the forms in the box to discuss these questions:

1 What things do visitors to your country find it difficult to get used to?

2 Compare school life with working life. What are students used to doing? What do people starting their first job have to get used to?

4 Finish each of these sentences in such a way that it means exactly the same as the sentence printed before it.

1 Juliet finds it strange driving on the left.
She's not ____________________

2 I always get up early, so it's not a problem.
I'm used ____________________

3 People in my country usually have quite a big meal at lunchtime.
They're used ____________________

4 Drinking a lot of tea is new for me.
I'm ____________________

5 After two or three days, you don't notice the cold weather so much.
It takes two or three days ____________________

LISTENING 1

This is Carole, who is 22 and works for a large company. Carole has come back to her old school to talk about her experiences of work to students who are in their last year of school.

1 What job do you think she does?

2 What questions do you think the students will want to ask her?
Listen to the talk and make a note of the students' questions.

3 Listen again and complete the missing information about Carole.

Her job: ....

Her original ambition: ....

Qualifications: 'A' Levels ....

.... Geography ....

Other languages: ....

Training: ....

Skills developed: ....

Hours worked: ....

Things which cause problems in her job:

.... Strikes, Overbooking, ...

....

Pay: ....

GRAMMAR GR p178

Present Perfect

1 Look at these phrases which Carole used to talk about her job, and answer the questions.

I've learned how to sort out those problems
The languages have been useful in my job
I've had lots of experience of dealing with people
I've had the chance to develop my interpersonal skills

1 When did these things happen?
2 Which tense did Carole use?
3 Why?

2 Look at these phrases which Carole used to talk about school, and answer the questions.

I never really liked school
I didn't work very hard
I liked the teachers in the sixth form
I enjoyed my A level subjects

1 When did these things happen?
2 Which tense did Carole use?
3 Why?

Look at this diagram:

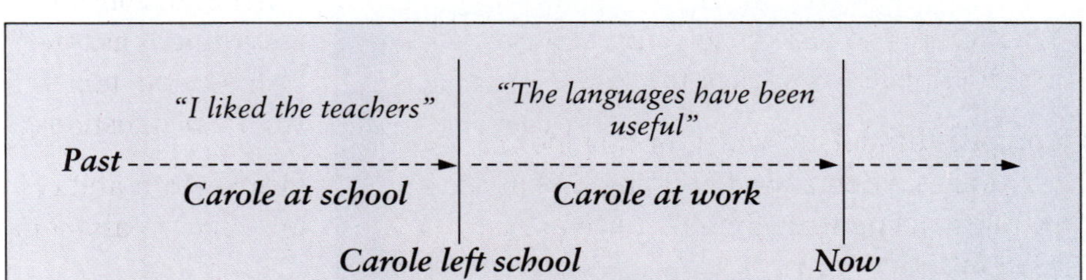

Carole uses a different tense to talk about these two periods in her life because one has finished and one has not.

The **Present Perfect** tense is used to talk about:		
	Tense	Time
Experiences		
I've been to London four times	Present Perfect	in my life
I've seen that film already	Present Perfect	in my life
Things that have happened in this period		
I've worked hard today	Present Perfect	today
I've done lots of sport this week	Present Perfect	this week
Things which have just or recently happened		
They've just arrived	Present Perfect	this moment
I've seen him twice recently	Present Perfect	recently

Compare this with the **Past** tense, which is used to talk about things which happened in periods which have finished.

	Tense	Time
I've been to Greece three times	Present Perfect	in my life
I went to Greece last year	Past	last year
I haven't seen him today	Present Perfect	today
I didn't see him on Sunday	Past	on Sunday

3 Look at the expressions in the box.

1 Divide them into those which talk about a present period and those which talk about a past period.

2 Choose four expressions from each list and write full sentences about your own educational or work experience.

when I was a child
last month
at Easter
last tuesday
in recent weeks
two weeks ago
in February
for the last 3 weeks
an hour ago
this century
last week
this month
since Christmas
since I left school

4 Put the verb in brackets into the correct tense, Present Perfect (I have done) or Past Simple (I did).

Examples: I *started* (start) working here last week.
I *have enjoyed* (enjoy) meeting you all today.

1 He ________ (pass) his exams last June.
2 She ________ (meet) her friend on Tuesday.
3 He ________ (learn) to type when he was at school.
4 She ________ (be) busy all this week.
5 Someone ________ (phone) you a few minutes ago.
6 He ________ (work) hard this term.
7 There ________ (be) a lot of work to do recently.
8 I ________ (have) any training on the word processor.
9 The twentieth century ________ (see) many technological advances.
10 Computers ________ (become) more important during the nineteen eighties.

LISTENING 2

1 Listen to an interview at a job agency and complete the missing details on the form below.

Ace JOB AGENCY

Student/Temporary Job Application

Name: Lucy ________

Address: ________ Conway Street, Cambridge

Subject(s) Studied: ________

Skills:	Yes	No
Languages	☑	☐
Typing/WP	☐	☐
Driving	☐	☐
Sports	☐	☐

Other ________

____

____

Work Experience:	Yes	No
Waiter/Waitress	☐	☐
Cook	☐	☐
Shop Assistant	☐	☐
Office work	☐	☐
With children	☐	☐

Other ________

____

Types of work required ________ or ____

____

Full or Part time ________

2 Using the information from the interview discuss which job might be suitable for Lucy.

3 Write down the questions which Lucy will ask to get more information about the job you have chosen.

4 Decide who is student A and who is student B.
Student A should ask Lucy's questions.
Student B should answer them by inventing more information about the job.

Choose another job and change roles.

WAITER/KITCHEN ASSISTANT REQUIRED.
Seasonal vacancy. No previous experience necessary.
Suitable for student.
Must be able to work under pressure and for long hours. Languages useful.

Full time plus some weekend work.
Good pay and tips.
Telephone: 342605

Research Assistant
required by university professor writing book on Mozart.
Some musical knowledge desirable.
Must be able to type. Driver preferred.
4 month vacancy. Would suit student.
Office hours. **Tel: 342898**

POST CARD
FOR SALE
FULL SIZE TABLE TENNIS TABLE.
NEARLY NEW - ONLY USED TWICE.
£75 O.N.O. RING GEOFF ON 342010

Helper for friendly village hotel required.
Early mornings and lunchtimes only.
Reception work, answering the phone, dealing with enquiries, handling money.
Some typing. **Summer vacancy.**
Suitable for flexible student.
Pay plus breakfast & lunch.
TEL: 342411

LOST!
BLACK + WHITE CAT, 2YRS OLD
ANSWERS TO THE NAME OF "SMUDGE".
LAST SEEN THURSDAY EVENING IN MARTEN LANE.
REWARD £10.00
PLEASE CONTACT JANE JACKSON
342979

Children's Nanny required for 2 months. Full time help for 4 lovely kids, includes a month with the family in a villa near Rome. Must be able to drive. No pay, but a great experience!
Tel: 342220

READING

1 Below is an article from a magazine about May, a student from Hong Kong.

1 Apart from the English language, what subjects do foreign students go abroad to study?
2 Why do they do this?
3 What are the advantages and disadvantages of studying in a foreign country?
4 Read and find out:
A what subject May is studying.
B how the course is organised.
C what her special interest is.

Name: May Lin, 20
Position: Industrial trainee
Qualifications *(pending):* BSc Hons Hotel and Catering Management
Company: Far East Enterprises
Institution: Norfolk Polytechnic, UK
Entry requirements: Minimum 2 A Levels

Currently in the third year of her Hotel and Catering Management course, May Lin was one of 70 young people to take up places in her year at Norfolk. She is now one of a remaining 55. There is no doubt that training in hospitality management can be arduous, she says.

"Those who dropped out did so because it was too hard, too long or because they no longer wanted to go into management."

The Norfolk course consists of a four year sandwich course; i.e. three years' study with a year's industrial placement midway. May chose to return to Hong Kong for her training, in order to practise her Cantonese, and found her own placement with Far East Enterprises.

Although she is working on a similar programme, she is not on the Enterprises' trainee programme and hence will not be offered a job at the end of it. But this suits her, as she has every intention of returning to complete her course. "I'm not sure yet where I want to work, and this way, I remain marketable in both Hong Kong and the UK."

She's very interested in restaurant/kitchen design, and has already won two major prizes for this in the UK. "I won first prize in British Gas' Eastern region award for kitchen design, and an award from Moderno Furniture for my restaurant furniture designs."

Her advice: "Learn English, and possibly another language as well, as many customers speak languages other than their own. It doesn't really matter which language – having another language could never be a disadvantage."

2 Match the words from the text on the left with the definitions on the right.

to take up (4)	therefore
arduous (9)	gave up
dropped out (10)	difficult
hence (27)	accept
award (40)	prize

3 Now answer these multiple-choice questions about the article.

1 Why did some people not complete the course?
   A They changed to another course.
   B There were too many students.
   C They did not pass the exams.
   D They found it too difficult.

2 What is May doing at the moment?
   A She is studying Cantonese at home.
   B She is working as part of her course.
   C She is looking for a job in Hong Kong.
   D She is on the Enterprises' trainee programme.

3 What will May do next year?
   A Learn another language.
   B Work as a furniture designer.
   C Return to Norfolk.
   D Find a job in Hong Kong.

4 What advice does she give?
   A Learn as many languages as possible.
   B Learn English and another language.
   C It is not important which languages you speak.
   D Keep practising your native language.

4 Look back at sections 1 – 3.

Why do you think some of the questions come before the reading passage and some after? How are the questions before the passage different from those which follow?

HELP WITH READING

Multiple choice questions

1 Look back at section 3. Choose a question which you answered correctly.
Now decide:

1 What is a multiple-choice question?
2 How did you choose the correct answer?
3 What is the purpose of the other three answers?
4 Why are they wrong?
5 Did you have any doubts? Why?

2 When answering multiple-choice questions there are important points to remember:

1 Read carefully and slowly to be sure you understand exactly what the passage says.

2 Look at the questions and try to answer them without looking at the alternatives. Try not to read all the alternatives until you have decided the answer in your own mind. Then find the alternative which is closest to your answer.

3 Some of the alternatives may seem logical or true but be careful not to introduce your own ideas. Look back at the passage to find the exact place where you can find the answer and make sure it really says what you think it says.

4 When you have decided, look at the alternatives and decide why each one is wrong.

LISTENING 3

You will hear a discussion between two people who work in the personnel department of a large company in London. They have just finished interviewing three applicants for the job described in the advertisement below.

1 Read the advertisement, then listen and complete the grid below with notes about the applicants.

Conference *organiser*

This is a great opportunity to use your organisational and interpersonal skills in an interesting and demanding role. As Conference Organiser you will quickly take responsibility for organising part of our busy conference programme. The job requires a lot of common sense, good administrative and communication skills, and ability to work as part of a team. Word processing skills and a driving licence are essential, experience of computer graphics desirable.

	Strong points	Weak points
Terry		
Pattie		
Jack		

2 Listen again and complete these sentences with the names of the job applicants (Terry, Pattie or Jack) using information from the grid.

1. _______ isn't as smart as _______.
2. _______ has got much more experience of computers than _______.
3. _______ doesn't have as much experience of organising conferences as _______.
4. I think _______ seemed more able to cope than _______.
5. _______ was much smarter than _______.
6. _______ has certainly got more experience of organising conferences than _______.

GRAMMAR *GR p178*

Comparatives

1 Divide the adjectives in the box into three groups according to how the comparative is formed.

enthusiastic	calm	old
tidy	able	nervous
reliable	responsible	smart
dirty	young	sensible

2 Using verbs from the box, write sentences about Terry, Pattie and Jack to show how each type of comparative adjective is formed.

3 Look at the information about Paul and Susie, two applicants for a job. Use the information to write six negative comparative sentences.

Example: Susie is not *as old as Paul.*

4 Finish each of the following sentences in such a way that it means exactly the same as the sentence printed before it.

1 Mandy has more experience than Sally.
Sally doesn't ____________________

2 Patrick is certainly more punctual than David.
David isn't ____________________

3 John isn't as well qualified as Sally.
Sally is ____________________

4 Juliet is more polite than Jill.
Jill isn't ____________________

5 My interview lasted longer than yours.
Your ____________________

Paul

Age: 26
Experience: 2 years
Attitude: very enthusiastic
Personality: excitable, sociable, talkative
Dress: untidy-not very smart

Susie

Age: 24
Experience: 5 years
Attitude: not very enthusastic
Personality: calm, serious, quiet, reserved
Dress: very smart and tidy

GRAMMAR
Infinitive vs because

1 Read the letter and answer these questions.

1 Why is Marie writing to John?
2 Why does Melanie want to stay in England?
3 Why does she need a job?
4 Why has Melanie got experience of working with children?
5 Why is Marie asking John to help?

2 How many of your answers did you begin with the word *because*?

1 Is *because* always the answer to *why*?
2 Does Marie use *because* in the letter?
3 Which form does she use in line 3 of the letter?
4 Now answer the questions again. How many of them can be answered using this form?

3 Which of the following questions can be answered with an infinitive and which need an explanation with *because*?

1 Why are you studying English?
2 Why are you studying for First Certificate?
3 Why do British people go on holiday to the Mediterranean?
4 Why is Greece hotter than Britain in the summer?
5 Why do people have to work?
6 Why don't people usually work on Sundays?
7 Why do some people earn more money than others?

4 When do we use the infinitive as an answer to some questions beginning with *why*?

84 Park Road
Newport

3rd February

Dear John,

Thank you very much for your letter, it was lovely to hear all about your new job.

I am writing to ask you a favour. A friend of mine, Melanie, is living in England at the moment. She is studying at a language school in London. Her course finishes in two weeks, but she would like to stay in England to do her First Certificate exam.

Do you know anybody who needs a babysitter or someone to help with the housework? Melanie is free every day after lunch and at the weekends, and she needs to earn some money to pay for her new course.

Melanie is a very nice, nineteen year-old girl from Holland. She has experience of looking after children and has worked as an au pair in Canada. She has her own flat so doesn't need any help with accommodation.

I'm sure you can help because you know so many people,

Thanks very much.

love,

Marie.

HELP WITH WRITING

Letter from Notes

1 Look at this sentence from Marie's letter.

I write/ask/you/favour.

1 Which words have been taken out?

2 Are there any other changes?

In the exam you may have to write a letter from notes in this way.

It is a good idea to read all of the letter first and decide what type of letter it is before you begin. These exercises will help you.

The letters in the exam generally fall into two categories:

Formal: To someone you do not know or a company.
Informal: To a friend or a member of your family.

2 **1** Think of four reasons why you might write a formal letter.

2 Think of four reasons why you might write an informal letter.

3 In this exercise, each sentence comes from a different letter. First, decide which type of letter each one comes from, then complete the sentences.

1 I/write/answer/advertisement/part-time staff/today/newspaper.

2 I/write/ask/you/like/come/party/Saturday night.

3 We have/lovely time/here/seaside.

4 Unfortunately/when/home/opened/box/piece/missing.

5 I enclose cheque/£4.50/which/include/£1.50/postage/packing.

6 It be/nice/birthday surprise/ever have.

4 Look at the first sentence of this letter.

Example: I write/ask information/your school.
I am writing to ask for information about your school.

1 Is this letter formal or informal?
2 What is the purpose of the letter?
3 What type of language does this type of letter usually contain?
4 Which grammatical tenses does this type of letter usually contain?
5 Is it the type of letter that usually contains question forms? Watch out for the question marks(?).

5 Write the complete letter from notes. Read everything before you begin.

Dear Mr. Smith,

I am writing to ask for information about your school.

I hope/come/Cambridge/three months/prepare/First Certificate exam.

1 ______________________________

I like/follow/course/only/mornings/as/I like/spend/afternoons/visit/city.

2 ______________________________

You organise/accommodation/me/family/so/get/conversation practice?

3 ______________________________

I study/English/five years/school/very good results.

4 ______________________________

I be/England/twice/summer courses/Brighton/I have/good reports/the school.

5 ______________________________

You think/I pass/First Certificate exam?

6 ______________________________

I look forward/hear/you/information/school/and/fees.

7 ______________________________

Yours sincerely
Monica Redoni

REVISION TEST 2

1 Listen to this extract from a radio programme.

The first time you listen answer questions 1–3.

1 What is the main problem with office work?
2 Why do most office workers not change their jobs?
3 What is the main advantage of working from home?

Listen again and answer these multiple choice questions on the same passage.

4 The main problem with office work is that
- A you have to work regular hours.
- B you can only work as a clerk or typist.
- C you have to do uninteresting work.
- D you have to work very hard.

5 Most office workers don't change their jobs because
- A they like the long holidays.
- B they don't have the opportunity.
- C they earn more in the office.
- D office work is comfortable and easy.

6 What is the main advantage of working from home?
- A It is easy to find work.
- B It is more comfortable than the office.
- C You can choose your own working hours.
- D It is financially secure.

2 The word in capitals at the end of each of the following sentences can be used to form a word that fits suitably in the blank space. Fill in each blank in this way.

Examples: His new job is very *stressful*.	STRESS
If you want the job, fill in this *application* form.	APPLY
1 He is a very ________ driver.	SKILL
2 Her desk is so ________ that she can never find what she wants.	TIDY
3 My teacher ________ me to enter this profession.	COURAGE
4 Copies of letters are kept in the ________ cabinet.	FILE
5 At the end of the course she was ________ a first-class Diploma.	AWARD

3 Complete each of the following phrases by putting one preposition in each of the spaces.

Example: The papers are urgent. You should act *on* them immediately.

1 20% of those who took ________ places on the course have now dropped ________.
2 He's worked there three years. He should put ________ for promotion.
3 If you would like a student travel card you have to fill ________ a green form.
4 When you've read that letter pass it ________ to John please.
5 Please tidy ________ your desks and throw ________ any documents you have had for more than six months.

4 Choose from these compositions:

1 What are the advantages and disadvantages of working with food?
2 What can be said for and against working in an office?

5 Make all the changes and additions necessary to produce, from the following sets of words and phrases, sentences which together make a complete letter. Note carefully from the example what kind of alterations need to be made. Write each sentence in the space provided.

Example: I write/ask/you/favour.
I am writing to ask you a favour.

A friend/mine/Melanie/living/England/moment.

1 ____

She study/language school/London.

2 ____

The course/finish/two weeks/she like/stay/England/take/First Certificate exam.

3 ____

You know/somebody/needs/babysitter/or someone help/housework?

4 ____

Melanie/free/every day/after lunch/weekends.

5 ____

She need/earn/money/pay/course.

6 ____

Melanie/very nice/nineteen year old/girl/Holland.

7 ____

She have/experience/look after/children/and work/au pair/Canada.

8 ____

She have/own flat/so not need help/accommodation.

9 ____

(The full letter can be found on page 29. Check to see if you remembered correctly.)

UNIT 3

HOME AND AWAY

VOCABULARY

(2)

(1)

(3)

(4)

1 Look at the photographs. Which of these places would you prefer to live in? Why? Do any of them look like your home?

2 Match each of the photographs with one of the descriptions.

A There are fantastic views from the balcony of this modern, one-bedroomed, sixth-floor flat. The luxury block has a resident porter and private underground garage.

B For a larger family, or a gardening enthusiast, this detached house is ideal. It has five bedrooms and is surrounded by a beautiful mature garden which also guarantees complete privacy.

C If you are looking for three good-sized bedrooms and an easy-to-maintain garden, this semi-detached house is perfect for you. It has recently been extensively modernised and has a double garage attached.

D This delightful country cottage is the perfect place to escape from the stresses of city life at the weekends. The inside of the house has been completely rebuilt, while the outside keeps its traditional appearance.

E Few homes in the centre of the town are as comfortable as this well-kept Victorian terraced house. There is a small garden at the front of the house and a sunny patio at the back.

F There are no stairs to climb or clean in this suburban bungalow. It has a medium-sized garden and a garage, but needs some modernisation.

3 In each description underline the one or two words which give a name to the type of home described. Description A has been done as an example.

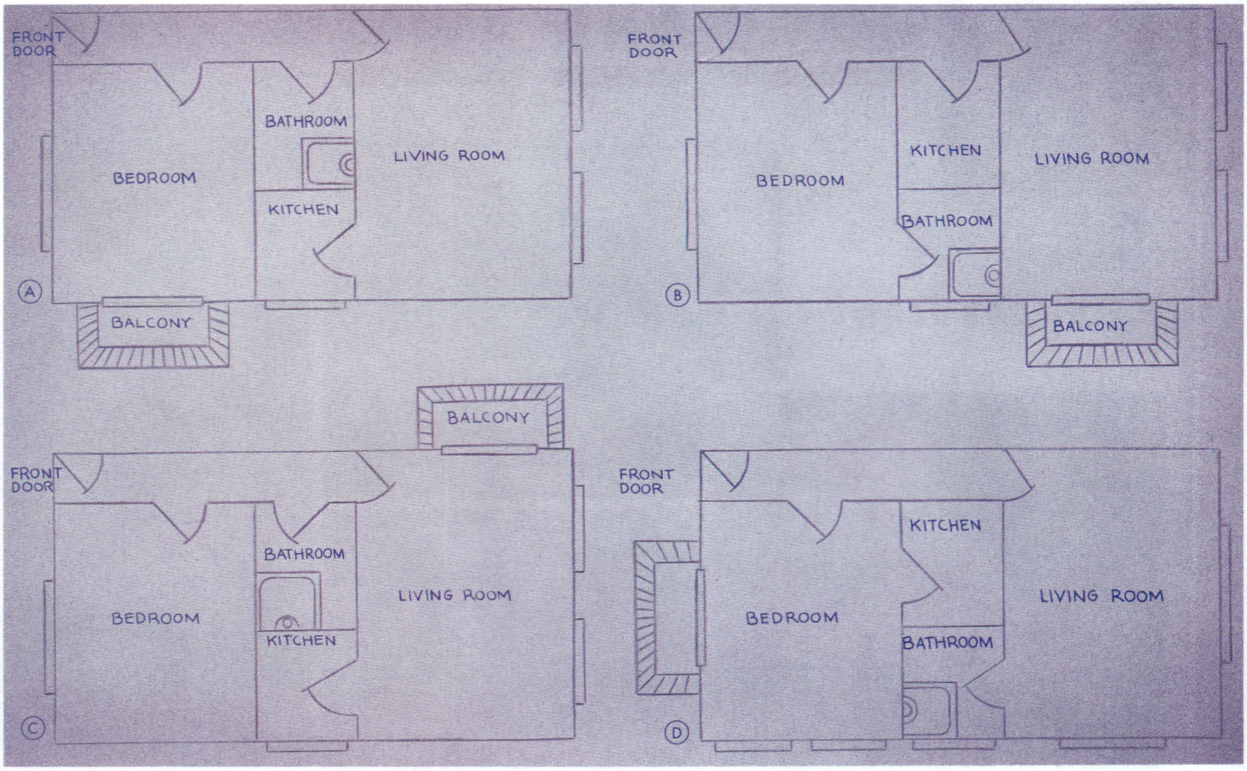

LISTENING 1.1

1 Listen to this telephone conversation and decide which of the four flats above, A, B, C or D is being described.

2 Listen again and tick (✓) the boxes to show which of these things the flat has got.

	yes	no	not mentioned
lift			
balcony			
phone			
shower			
bath			
garage			
cooker			
fridge			
central heating			

LISTENING 1.2

Listen to the conversation and complete Sharon's notepad.

things that need doing	do it myself	have it done
bathroom needs cleaning		
windows need (1) ______	✓	
(2) ______ needs changing		
(3) ______ ______ need repainting		
light switches need (4) ______		✓
(5) ______ ______ needs (6) ______		✓
(7) ______ rail needs (8) ______ ______		

GRAMMAR GR p178

Causative Have/Needs Doing

1 Look at these phrases from the listening text.
I'm having a new lock fitted
I'll have it done professionally

1 Who is going to do the work?
To have something done ('causative have') is formed by:

the subject	= Sharon
the verb *to have*	= is having
the object	= her central heating
the past participle of the main verb	= serviced

= *Sharon is having her central heating serviced.*

This means that somebody is servicing Sharon's central heating for her.

Compare with:
Sharon is servicing her central heating.

This means that Sharon is doing the work herself.

2 Match a 'causative have' sentence in **A** with its equivalent in **B** and the tense in **C**.

A
1 I have my newspaper delivered.
2 I'm having my newspaper delivered.
3 I've had my newspaper delivered.
4 I had my newspaper delivered.

B
5 Somebody delivered my newspaper for me.
6 Somebody delivers my newspaper for me.
7 Somebody has delivered my newspaper for me.
8 Somebody is delivering my newspaper for me.

C
9 Present Continuous
10 Present Perfect
11 Present Simple
12 Past Simple

Notice that in the causative it is the verb *to have* which tells us the tense.

3 Needs Doing

'Your dog needs looking after!'

2 Match each verb in the box with one of the pictures.

feed	exercise	clip
groom	wash	train

3 Use one of the verbs to complete each of the following sentences about the dog.

Example: This dog is too thin, it needs *feeding* properly.

1 This dog looks untidy, it needs ________ regularly.
2 This dog is very dirty, it needs ________ thoroughly.
3 This dog's coat is too long, it needs ________ professionally.
4 This dog is lazy, it needs ________ daily.
5 This dog is badly behaved, it needs ________ properly.

4 What can you have done to your dog at Dogsbody?

Example: You can have your dog fed.

Dogsbody

Full Pet Service
By Qualified Person

Anything from Hamsters to Horses.
Feeding. Exercise. Loving care and attention.

Dog clipping & grooming
(D.G. Diploma CSI)

All Breeds

Show ring training

Phone Joyce or Lesley on 0224 440921

5 With your partner discuss what you can have done in each of these places. Use the verbs in the box to help you.

A the hairdresser's
B the dentist's
C the garage

A	B	C
cut	fill	change
perm	take out	repair
shampoo	clean	check
dry	check	service
dye	X-ray	replace

6 Finish each of the following sentences in such a way that it means exactly the same as the sentence printed before it.

1 A shop mended my vacuum cleaner for me.
I had ______________________________
2 I took my car to a garage to be washed.
I had ______________________________
3 Someone came and repaired the broken window in my house.
I ______________________________
4 A servant prepares all his meals.
He ______________________________
5 A famous designer makes all her clothes.
She has ______________________________

SPEAKING

1 Discuss with your partner:
Have you ever stayed as a guest in someone else's house?
What are the good points and bad points about staying away from home?
Have you ever had a guest staying in your house?
What are the good points and bad points about having guests?

2 Decide with your partner who is student A and who is student B. Read the instructions below.

Student A Think of 5 things you should do when you are a guest in someone's house and 5 things you shouldn't do. Use the topics in the box to help you.

Student B Think of 5 things you should do when you have a guest in your house and 5 things you shouldn't do. Use the topics in the box to help you.

meals	television	sleeping	furniture
bathroom	kitchen	music	telephone

Now discuss the things with your partner.

READING

foreign **exchange**

Hotels and tourist trips don't always give you the freedom to enjoy a holiday the way you want it. Why not swap your home with another family and find out what life is really like in your dream destination?

A change may be as good as a rest, but when it comes to holidays, more and more people are discovering that home exchange – swapping your house with another family – is a good deal better than a package.

For a start, it's a financial winner. Compared with the daunting cost of even the most reasonable fortnight in the sun in a hotel or rented apartment, you will be paying literally nothing for accommodation.

There's also the pleasantly reassuring feel that both houses are therefore occupied and not an open invitation to burglars and vandals.

And instead of a soulless hotel, you are part of a genuine community, probably with your host's friends and neighbours helping to make you welcome.

If both families have children they will make local friends – and have the run of the resident toy cupboard. Experienced swappers agree that living as guests in someone else's house encourages mutual respect for each other's property – although it is probably sensible to pack away vulnerable treasures.

Some of the most successful home-swap holidays have made firm friends of the families involved – with the children becoming pen pals and even getting together to organise their own combined holidays in subsequent years.

1
1. What do you think are the advantages of swapping homes with another family from a different country as a holiday?
2. Are there any disadvantages or dangers?
3. Read the first part of the article and list the main advantages it mentions.
4. Are any disadvantages mentioned?
5. Decide who is student A, B and C. Part Two of the article is divided into three parts: A, B and C. Each of you should read one part. Follow your instructions on the next page.

…nt A
Read Part **A** and find this information:
What two ways of making contact are mentioned?
What do you give to the agency? What can the agency do for you?

Student B
Read Part **B** and find this information:
What are some important things to do once you have found a family who want to swap?
What information could be useful to the family?

Student C
Read Part **C** and find this information:
What should you arrange or provide for the guest family before they arrive?
What should the guest family do before they leave?

Part A

Finding your match

How do you set about house swapping? Unless you can make your own arrangements privately through friends and contacts, the most practical way is to use one of the specialist agencies who put potential clients in touch with each other, either around the UK or worldwide. These companies differ in the services they offer, but in most cases you pay a registration fee (from £15 upwards) to be included in a directory which is then circulated to prospective swappers in the country of your choice.

In some cases you will be asked to fill in a comprehensive form, listing everything about your home from the number of beds and bathrooms to whether there are pets to look after or plants to water. There will usually be a photograph of your house in the directory – and perhaps also of your family – as well as the holiday dates you have in mind and your particular preferences as to location: town, country, seaside and so on.

Some agencies just put families in touch through their directories and thereafter leave all the arrangements to you; others will visit and vet individual properties, taking trouble to match each family's requirements, and some will also arrange air travel for you – and obviously charge accordingly.

Part B

Making contact

Once you've received your directory and settled on some 'possibles' you like the look of, it's sensible to write at once to several of them; all agencies stress the importance of getting your holiday arrangements made well in advance.

Having made initial contact with 'your' family, you should start to establish a relationship by post or, if practical, by telephone. You can then exchange photos and appropriate information.

When it comes to preparing for your guests, remember that they will be holidaying in a strange place, so it's worth spending time putting together an information folder with phone numbers for emergency services, doctor, police and so on, as well as details of local shops, restaurants, travel timetables and availability of baby-sitters. Include any instructions they may find useful for dealing with pets, houseplants or refuse collection. If you have a burglar alarm or complicated kitchen equipment, leave clear how-to-use details. It's also a good idea to contact your local tourist office for brochures on excursions, stately homes, theme parks and other local interests, so that you can leave your visitors with plenty of ideas for things to do and places to see.

Part C

Changing places

Unless one family plans to arrive before the other has left, it's vital that you make failsafe arrangements for someone to meet the new arrivals, hand over the keys and make them welcome. In any case, do ask your neighbours to take a helpful interest. It's a nice idea to leave some basic provisions for the first couple of meals and perhaps a bottle of wine, but don't overcater by filling the freezer and inviting them to help themselves; part of the fun of a holiday is exploring local shops and cooking 'foreign' food, and although you may not think of your local Co-Op as a treasure house of rare delicacies, it could well seem so to your guests.

Remember, too, if cars are included in the swap, to make sure that insurance arrangements cover everything, and that there is petrol in the tank. It's usual for services such as gas and electricity to be paid by the host family in each case, but any extra expenses such as long-distance telephoning should be settled up before the end of the holiday.

The departing family should also make sure they leave the house exactly as they found it, and replenish dwindling stocks of household goods such as loo paper or light bulbs. And a vase of flowers' (not from the host's garden!) with a thank-you note will show your appreciation to the returning owner.

2

1 Find some other students in the class who have read the same part of the article and compare your answers.
2 Now find partners who have each read different parts. Exchange information.
3 Complete these four paragraphs in your own words to summarise the article.

A Exchanging houses is a good idea for holidays because ____________________

B The best way of contacting a family is ________ because ____________________

C Once you've contacted a family you should ____________________

D Before your guest family arrives you should ____________________

LISTENING 2

1 Listen to this phone call between two friends who haven't heard from each other for a long time and complete the details below.

New address ____________________

Type of house ____________________

Reason for moving ____________________

How long has Margaret lived there? ______

How long has Peter lived there? _________

How long has Margaret known Peter? ____

2 Now look at these phrases from the listening text.

I haven't heard from you for ages
No, we haven't talked since Christmas

When do we use *for* and when do we use *since*?

GRAMMAR GR p179

For/Since

1 Put *for* or *since* in each of the following phrases:

1 We haven't invited Auntie Joan ________ years.
2 I haven't seen him ________ his birthday.
3 I've lived here ________ I was a child.
4 I've had my new car ________ three months.
5 I've had this watch ________ longer than I can remember.
6 I've been there six times ________ I came back from my holidays.

2 Look at these three sentences. Which of these sentences is different grammatically? In what way is it different?

1 I haven't seen him for ages.
2 It's ages since I saw him.
3 I haven't seen him since Christmas.

HELP WITH GRAMMAR

Transformation sentences

1 Part of the Use of English paper asks you to transform sentences from one grammatical structure to another. You are given a complete sentence:

Example: I haven't had such fun for years.

This is followed by an incomplete sentence:

It's ______________________________

The example is completed like this:

It's *years since I had so much fun.*

The new sentence must mean exactly the same as the original, but will probably use a different grammatical structure.

2 Look at this transformation:

She left school five years ago.

It's *five years since she left school.*

1 What has changed? Why?
2 What has not changed? Why not?
3 What has been omitted?
4 What has been added?

3 Are these examples of good transformations?

Example: He didn't arrive in time to meet her.

a He arrived *too late to meet her.*
b He arrived *early enough to meet her.*

Answer: a is a good transformation because in the original sentence the meeting DID NOT take place because he was late. b is grammatically correct but is not a good transformation because the meaning has changed.

Example: John is the best footballer in the club.

a No one *in the club plays football as well as John.*
b No one *in the club plays football better than John.*

Answer: Both are correct. They both mean that John is the best.

For questions 1 – 5 decide whether a and b are good transformations or not.

1 I can't drive as well as my father.
a My father *drives as well as I do.*
b My father *drives better than I do.*

2 The water was so cold it was impossible to have a shower.
a The water *was too cold for us to have a shower.*
b The water *wasn't warm enough for us to have a shower.*

3 She liked London much more than Cambridge.
a She didn't *like Cambridge as much as London.*
b She didn't *like Cambridge or London either.*

4 I always have breakfast before I leave the house.
a I don't *leave the house before I have had breakfast.*
b I don't *leave the house until I have had breakfast.*

5 Let's go swimming.
a Why *don't we go swimming*?
b Why *should we go swimming*?

4 Finish each of the following sentences in such a way that it means exactly the same as the sentence printed before it.

1 It's weeks since I received a letter.
I haven't ______________________________

2 I haven't eaten in a restaurant for months.
It's ______________________________

3 Dogsbody washed my dog for me.
I had ______________________________

4 The newspaper hasn't been delivered for two days.
It's ______________________________

5 Somebody cleaned Lidia's house for her before the guests arrived.
Lidia ______________________________

LISTENING 3

1 Look at this wedding photograph.
Describe the people.
Could this be a wedding in your country?
What would be the same or different?

2 You will hear part of a radio phone-in programme where people ask an expert for advice on etiquette at weddings.
Listen to Part 1 and complete the information in the grid below.
Student A should listen for Mrs Romsey's questions, and Student B for the answers.

Mrs Romsey's questions	*The answers*
Should I make the guest list or should my daughter?	Bride's parents can choose the guests.
Ought I to ask for suggestions?	You should ______ ______
Is it alright if ______ ______?	You should ______
What should I ______ ______?	You could ask ______
Can I ______ ______?	Yes, if ______

3 You will hear some more callers on the line to the same programme.
For Parts 2, 3 and 4:
a Decide what the problem is.
b Discuss with your partner what advice would be appropriate in your country.
c Listen to see if the expert's advice is the same as yours or different.

READING

1 Discuss:

1 How do you show your appreciation when someone gives you a gift?
What do you say?
What do you do?
2 What do you say if someone gives you a present you don't like?
3 Do you ever write letters to say thank you?
4 In what situation do you think a letter of thanks might be appropriate?

modern MANNERS

1 I remember, when I was about seven, agonising over how to thank my Aunt Pat for the excruciatingly awful jumper she'd sent me for my birthday. It was three sizes too big and a horrible mixture of brightly coloured wools. Needless to say I wasn't very happy about wearing it, still I was obliged to put pen to paper and be thankful in writing. But my parents had taught me not to lie and I was totally honest about what I was going to do with the present:

Dear Aunt Pat
thank you very much for the jumper. It is very big. there are many COld children in the world who do not get presents I will donate it to the OxForm Shop
love.
Michele

2 My parents' philosophy of manners didn't extend to being that honest, so the note was altered before being posted:

Dear Aunt Pat
thank you for the jumper it is rally very nice of you to knitit for me. It must have taken a very very long time
thank you.
Love
Michele

3 But where do we stand on an old fashioned concept like thank you letters, when we live in a modern world of cordless phones and motorways that take us to Granny's and back in a day?

4 In any era, there should be good, solid reasons for asking our children to do things – and, for me, that's the hard bit ... working out the reasons and explaining them.

5 Some 'traditions' make sense to me – like saying 'please' and 'thank you' because it makes other people feel good, or giving up your seat on the bus to someone less able because it's kind. Some don't make sense – like children not speaking until spoken to. It seems to me that we need to work things out as we go along.

6 So, what about those thank you notes? In fact, I do usually make my boys write them when presents come by post. One reason is that receiving a thank you note in a world of ever-ringing phones is special, and makes the recipient feel special; and because grandparents, especially, like to re-read notes, and show them to friends.

7 There's another reason, too, that's hard to define. I think it's because sitting down to write focuses your thoughts and the result is a little part of yourself that's unique (provided you didn't copy it from your sister).

8 Remembering my own struggles, I do try to make it easier on my children. It's hard to think kind thoughts when you're oppressed. So picture postcards make good thank you notes. You can let the child choose one from some you have bought – and even address and stamp it for them. Older children can write a few lines; younger ones can just write 'thank you' and sign their name. Even little ones can draw a picture of themselves playing with the gift.

2 Read the article by Michele Elliot to find the answers to the following questions. Underline the parts of the text where you find the answers.

1 Why didn't Michele like the present from her auntie?
2 Why didn't her parents like her first letter?
3 Which other two traditions does she agree with and why?
4 When does she make her sons write thank-you letters?
5 What are the three reasons she gives for sending a note rather than using the phone?
6 What advice does she give parents about how to make letter-writing easier for young children?

Now compare your answers with your partner's. Do you both agree with Michele?

3 Look at the article again and find:

1 Two words meaning the same as 'pullover' and a verb describing how these are made.
2 A phrase which means 'obviously' (paragraph 1).
3 A phrase which means 'to write' (paragraph 1).
4 A verb meaning 'changed' (paragraph 2).
5 A phrase meaning 'what is our opinion' (paragraph 3).

WRITING

An informal letter

1 Look at the letter on page 29. This is an example of an *informal* letter.

How do you know it is an informal letter?

Look at: the address.
the first words of the letter (the greeting).
the content (the topics included in the letter).
the concluding words (the close).
the name at the end of the letter.

All of these things can help you decide if a letter is informal or formal.

2 Carol has been invited to spend the weekend with Tim. She is writing to refuse the invitation and make some other suggestions. The beginning and the end of the letter are complete. Put the middle paragraph into the correct order.

37 Castle Street
Manchester
M20 2BA

4th May

Dear Tim,

Thank you very much for inviting me to come and stay with you for the weekend.

a would that be OK?
b as there isn't much traffic,
c I'd love to come and visit you,
d How about if I just came for the day on Sunday,
e and I can come home late in the evening.
f but I'm afraid I'm very busy at this time of year
g Getting to your house on a Sunday morning is easy
h and I don't think I can be away for a whole weekend.

Please let me know if this plan is alright. Maybe we can arrange a whole weekend together later in the year. Then you can come and stay at my house, we've got lots of room and my family are always very pleased to see you.

Best wishes,

Carol

P.S. Can you send me Erica's phone number? I think I've lost it.

Address

25 Brighton Road
Keyworth
[illegible]

Date

4th May

Greeting

Dear Martha,

Thank you very much for your invitation to the birthday party next week.

I'm really sorry, but I'm afraid I won't be able to come. My Aunt Betty is coming with Dennis to visit us that weekend and we've got tickets for the ballet. I haven't seen them for years and I can't really cancel now.

I hope you and the boys have a lovely evening - I really wish I could join you. I'm thinking of organising a trip to the zoo in a couple of weeks and I immediately thought you'd be interested.

I'll give you a ring next week to sort something out.

Close

Best wishes,

Your name

3 You are unable to go to the party, and you write a letter. Be particularly careful to make sure your letter *looks* like an informal letter. Use the model on the right to guide you.

4 Write a letter to a friend you haven't seen for some time. Mention some recent news about yourself and people you both know.

REVISION TEST 3

1 For each question 1 to 10 choose the word or phrase which best completes the sentence.

1 Which is the ________ way to thank a guest for a gift?
A correctly B corrected C correction D correct

2 He ________ the invitation as he was busy that weekend.
A rejected B renounced C denied D refused

3 Their son's bad ________ is something I cannot put up with in my house.
A habit B training C behaviour D manner

4 Since I left England, I haven't had much ________ with my friends there.
A contact B relation C meeting D hearing

5 When he stays in her house he always complains ________ her dog.
A for B about C of D from

6 ________ to say, I wasn't happy about having that cat in my house.
A Needed B Needing C Needless D Needn't

7 The letter arrived ________ post.
A by B with C through D from

8 There should be good reasons for ________ children to do things.
A ask B asked C asking D to ask

2 The word in capital letters at the end of each of the following sentences can be used to form a word that fits suitably in the blank space. Complete each of the blanks in this way.

Example: When I was in the USA, I was impressed by the *hospitality* I received. HOSPITABLE

1 In your own home you have the __________ to behave as you wish. FREE
2 It is __________ to take some toys on the journey for the children to play with. ADVISE
3 I hate that __________ coloured pullover. BRIGHT
4 This iron is broken; it needs __________. MEND
5 I'm taking my car to the garage to have the brakes __________. CHECK

3 In sentences 1–5 fill in each of the blanks with one suitable word.

Example: Paul has a large number of uncles, aunts, cousins and other distant *relations*.

1 Alison has dogs, cats, goldfish and many other ________.
2 Which kind of ________ would you prefer? You can stay in a hotel, a guest house or with a family.
3 As a child I never ate cabbage, spinach, peas or other kinds of green ________.

4 Sandra was presented with a bouquet of roses, carnations, tulips and other beautiful ________.

5 Chris is a very good pianist, and can also play a number of other musical ________.

4 Fill in each of the numbered blanks in the following passage, which is a continuation of the article on page 42. Use ONE word only in each space.

Once I ________ (1) with an aunt who served me cooked carrots – a huge helping. They were overcooked, yellow ________ (2) disgusting. I tasted ________ (3) and then said no thank you. In that house, though, manners dictated that you eat what was on your ________ (4), even if you hadn't served yourself with it. There were starving children in Africa!

Believe it or not, I ________ (5) to sit at the table until bedtime. The ________ (6) morning the carrots reappeared on my breakfast plate. I was a stubborn little creature and never did eat them or stay with the aunt ________ (7). And I will not eat cooked carrots to this day. Children ________ (8) not be abused in the name of manners.

Since we want meal times to be a pleasure, I reckon the ________ (9) way is to put the food in serving dishes and let children help themselves. Have manners 'rules' that everyone agrees to, but above all ________ (10) meal times fun. If we are too strict, too critical, meal times become tense.

5 Finish each of the following sentences in such a way that it means exactly the same as the sentence printed before it.

Example: I haven't laughed so much for years.
It's years *since I laughed so much.*

1 Somebody repaired her bicycle last week.
She ________________________________

2 He is not strong enough to do that job.
He is too ________________________________

3 Keith is not as well qualified as Sue.
Sue ________________________________

4 I haven't spoken to Mr Williams before.
This is the ________________________________

5 Somebody is repainting our house at the moment.
We ________________________________

6 Linda hasn't got as much experience as Graham.
Graham ________________________________

7 The carpet still needs cleaning.
The carpet hasn't ________________________________

8 One advantage of living in the country is clean air.
One point in ________________________________

UNIT 4 WHODUNNIT?

VOCABULARY

1 What is a crime?
Match the crimes in the box below with their definitions 1–10.

1 stealing from shops while they are open
2 killing someone intentionally
3 stealing objects in general
4 breaking into buildings to steal things
5 attacking and hurting someone physically
6 making false documents
7 attacking someone and stealing from them in the street
8 stealing money from banks, etc.
9 taking someone prisoner and demanding money for their release
10 crimes such as illegal parking, speeding, etc.

burglary	shoplifting
murder	robbery
mugging	theft
minor offences	assault
forgery	kidnapping

2 What is the name for the people who commit each of these crimes?

Which is the most serious of these crimes?
Which is the most common in your country?
Which is the least common?

3 Look at the chart showing crime figures for a city in Britain for this year and last year. Use the words in the box to talk to your partner about how these figures have changed.

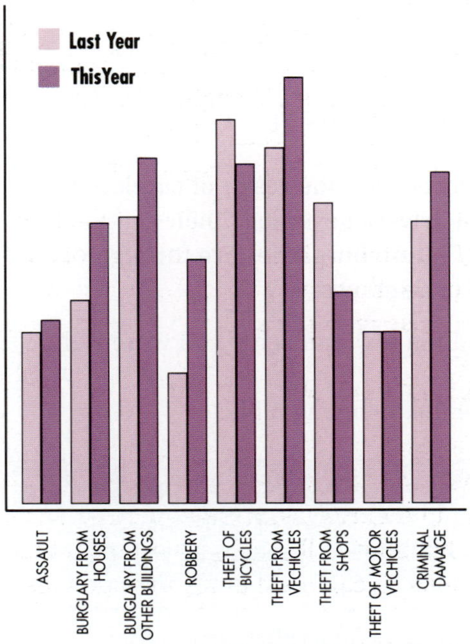

Crime figures for the last 12 months compared with those for the previous 12 months

↑	↓	↔
increased	decreased	stayed level
gone up	gone down	stayed the same
risen	fallen	not changed
doubled	halved	remained stable
climbed	dropped	

Example: The number of burglaries from houses has gone up in the last year.

4 How can we prevent crime
at home?
at school?
in other places?

READING

1 Look at the following statements about crimes in Britain, and say whether you think they are true or false.

1 Most crimes involve our possessions and not ourselves.
2 Most criminals make enough money from crime to live on.
3 Most criminals follow careful plans.
4 Most criminals are young people.
5 Most criminals give up crime after a few years.
6 Most crimes are the result of carelessness.
7 20% of drivers never lock their cars.
8 70% of house burglaries are through open doors or windows.

Now read the text and see if you were right.

2 Complete the following table:

Verb	Noun (action)	Noun (person)
to steal		thief
to rob	robbery	
to	burglary	burglar
to commit an offence	offence	
to	mugging	mugger

3 Now put the correct form of one of the words into each of the following sentences.

1 The police are looking for a gang which got away with £20,000 in a bank ________.
2 She came home to find her house had been ________ and her car ________.
3 A ________ broke into the school at night and took two video players.
4 Police are very concerned about the increase in ________ from parked cars.
5 The ________ knocked him to the ground and ran off with his briefcase.

Crime, as we are all aware, has been a growing problem all over the world in the last 30 years. But we are not powerless against crime. Much is being done — and more can be done — to reverse the trend. You can play a part in it.

The first step towards preventing crime is understanding its nature. Most crime is against property, not people. And most is not carried out by professionals; nor is it carefully planned. Property crimes thrive on the easy opportunity. They are often committed by adolescents and young men, the majority of whom stop offending as they grow older — the peak ages for offending are 15–18. Also and not surprisingly, the risk of crime varies greatly depending on where you live.

This reliance by criminals on the easy opportunity is the key to much crime prevention.

Motor cars, for example, are a sitting target for the criminal. Expensive, attractive and mobile, they are often left out on the streets for long periods at a time.

The police estimate that 70–90 per cent of car crime results from easy opportunities.

Surveys have shown that approximately one in five drivers do not always bother to secure their cars by locking all the doors and shutting all the windows.

It's the same story with our homes. In approximately 30 per cent of domestic burglaries, the burglar simply walks in without needing to use force; the householder has left a door unlocked or window open.

If opportunities like these did not exist, criminals would have a much harder time. The chances are that many crimes would not be committed at all, which would in turn release more police time for tackling serious crime.

Of course, the primary responsibility for coping with crime rests with the police and the courts. But there are many ways that you can help reverse the trend. So if you care about improving the quality of life for yourself, your family and your community, read on ...

LISTENING 1

You will hear someone telling a police officer about a break-in at her home. Listen and complete the missing information on the form below.

DATE: 17th June ____________ TIME: 17·45 ____________

NAME: ________________________________ (1)

ADDRESS: ________________________ (2) George Street

ESTIMATED TIME OF OFFENCE: ____________ (3)

ARTICLES MISSING:		VALUE:		IDENTIFICATION:	
____________	(4)	________	(5)	________________	(6)
____________	(7)	—		________________	(8)
____________	(9)	________	(10)		

DAMAGE: ________________________________ (11)

GRAMMAR GR p179

Past Simple/Continuous

1 Look at these phrases from the listening text, and for each one decide:

Which tenses are used.
Why each tense is used.

1 I got home and found the door open.
2 As I was walking along the road to my house I noticed that the front door was open.
3 My neighbour was cleaning her windows, so before I went in I called to her.
4 They got in while I was out shopping.

Look at the following examples of past tenses:

The **Past Simple** is used to talk about:	Tense	Time
Events in the past I went to London in 1990.	Past Simple	1990
Events that happened one after another I got home and made a cup of tea	Past Simple	one event, then another

The **Past Continuous** is used to talk about:	Tense	Time
Events beginning in the past but not finished at a specific time in the past		
My neighbour was washing her car	Past Continuous	when I got home
What were you doing at 8.00 pm last night?	Past Continuous	at 8.00 pm

The **Past Continuous** and **Past Simple** are used together:

a When one action is interrupted by another:

I was walking down the path when I noticed that the door was open.
While I was having a bath the phone rang.

b When one action takes place during a longer one:

When I was studying in Paris I visited The Louvre.
While I was living in London I went to the theatre regularly.

2 Change the verb in brackets into the Past Simple or Past Continuous.

1 I (phone) ________ my brother when the door bell (ring) ________.
2 He (live) ________ in London when the accident (happen) ________.
3 As it (rain) ________ we (decide) ________ to stay at home.
4 I (not hear) ________ the phone because I (sit) ________ in the garden.
5 They (break) ________ three plates while they (stay) ________ in my house.
6 They (do) ________ the washing up and then (go) ________ to the cinema.
7 When she (arrive) ________ Luke (play) ________ the guitar and Mary (read) ________ a book.
8 During her visit to Milan she (go) ________ skiing every weekend.

READING

1 Do you know anyone whose car has been stolen or broken into? Tell your partner what happened.
What can people do to protect their cars against this sort of crime?
Make a list of suggestions.
Compare with your partner.

2 Read the passage quickly and find out what these numbers refer to:

1 460,000
2 20
3 ¼

Apart from your home, your car is probably your most valuable possession.

It's also your most vulnerable.

KEEPING YOUR CAR SAFE

Car thefts and thefts from cars – typically of radios and cassette players – account for over a quarter of all recorded crime. Together they impose costs on everyone – the cost of the police time taken up in dealing with the offences, the cost of taking offenders through the criminal justice system, and the cost to motorists of increased insurance premiums.

Over 460,000 cars are reported missing in Britain each year and many of these are never recovered. Many of those which are found have been damaged by the thieves. A stolen car is also far more likely to be involved in an accident than the same car driven by its owner; car thieves are often young and sometimes drunk.

Yet car crime can be cut drastically if motorists follow a few simple rules to keep thieves out of their cars in the first place.

Most car thieves are opportunist unskilled petty criminals; many are under 20. So make your own car a less inviting target, to discourage thieves from trying.

3 Now read again and discuss the following questions with your partner. Underline the parts of the text where you find the answer.

1 How does car theft cost everyone money? (three things)
2 What often happens to cars that are stolen? (three things)
3 What sort of people are involved in this type of crime? (three answers)

LISTENING 2

Listen to two phone calls to a radio programme where a security expert is giving advice. Complete the missing information below.

First Caller:
Items stolen? ________ (1) and jewellery
Where from? ________ (2)
Expert's suggestions?
__________________________ (3)
__________________________ (4)

Second Caller:
Items stolen? ________________ (5)
Where from? ________________ (6)
Expert's suggestions?
__________________________ (7)
__________________________ (8)
__________________________ (9)

GRAMMAR GR p179

Deductions

1 Look at these sentences from the listening text.

1 *It might have been one of the waiters.*
2 *It could have been the people at the next table.*
3 *It must have been a very brave thief.*
4 *The doors can't have been locked.*

What time do the sentences refer to?
What tense is used?

2 Decide if each of the sentences from the text means either: it's one possible explanation or: it's the only explanation.

3 Read this passage from a crime novel and find the three important facts which the inspector knows about the crime.

> So, who killed Keith Thurbold? All four suspects seemed to have good alibis for the evening, but one of them found the time to kill Keith and dispose of the body.
>
> Inspector Skea looked again at the report in front of her. The medical evidence seemed to confirm everything that she had been thinking. The body was found at nine p.m. in the woods twelve miles from Raybury town centre, but the medical report put the time of death at between six and seven p.m. This was interesting. Each of the suspects had a car, and it would take about twenty minutes to drive those twelve miles along the small country roads on a normal day – but in the fog it may have taken longer.
>
> She picked up her list of suspects again and quickly looked through her notes – ah, yes, there it was. The answer she was looking for! She just had a couple more questions to ask one of the suspects, then she would have the murderer.

4 Look at Inspector Skea's notes on Agnes, Daphne, Marilyn and Derek, and decide if each of these people could have committed the murder, or not.

5 Write four paragraphs in your own words. Begin like this:

1 I don't think _______ can have been the murderer because _______
2 I think _______ might have been the murderer because _______
3 I think _______ could have been the murderer because _______
4 But, I think _______ must have committed the murder because _______

1 Agnes Thurbold

Address:	4 Linton Terrace, Raybury
Relationship:	sister
Motive:	family quarrel – they haven't spoken for years
Alibi:	
5.00	seen leaving the public library
5.10-6.15	alone at home, 'having dinner'
6.15	Mrs Jay (a friend) arrived
6.15-8.00	watched TV with Mrs Jay
8.00	took Mrs Jay home by car (10 mins)

2 Daphne Thurbold

Address:	12 Dorchester Gardens, Raybury.
Relationship:	wife (separated)
Motive:	waiting for divorce, could lose house and car
Alibi:	
5.00	left work
5.30	seen arriving home by neighbour
5.30-6.15	alone at home
6.15-6.30	on phone to daughter in America
6.30-7.25	alone at home, getting ready and driving to the theatre (5 mins)
7.25	arrived at Raybury theatre looking calm and elegant
7.25-9.45	in theatre with friends

3 Marilyn Morecott

Address:	14 Alexandra Road, Raybury.
Relationship:	girlfriend
Motive:	she will inherit his money and share in the business
Alibi:	
5.00	left work
5.30	met friend in town centre
6.30-8.00	in cinema with friend
8.15-9.30	in pizzeria with friend

4 Derek Morecott

Address:	The Bungalow, Carter's Lane, Raybury.
Relationship:	business partner, husband of Marilyn (separated)
Motive:	jealousy, revenge?
Alibi:	
5.45	left the office with Keith (secretary confirms)
6.30	arrived home alone (son confirms)
6.30-8.00	at home with son
8.00	son went out
8.00-8.40	at home alone
8.40-8.45	received phone call from London

VOCABULARY

Help with Guessing

When you are reading and you are not sure what words mean, it is possible to guess from the context. This is an important skill because in the exam you are not allowed to use a dictionary and you cannot ask anyone to explain vocabulary to you.

1 In the passage, the nonsense word 'spreg' has been used instead of some of the real words. For each one decide if 'spreg' is a noun, verb, adjective, adverb or another type of word. What do you think 'spreg' means in each example?
Is there more than one possible answer?

We got up early this morning and as it was a (1) *spreggy* day we went to the zoo to see the (2) *spregs*. We've (3) *spregged* the zoo many times recently as we are (4) *spregly* interested in (5) *spregs* and so we went to the (6) *spreg* house first.

We were very lucky. We (7) *spregged* just in (8) *spreg* to see them (9) *spregged*. It was (10) *spreg!*

Example:
1 *Word Type* – adjective
General Meaning – describes the weather
Possible Words – lovely, sunny, beautiful

2 Compare with your partner. Have conversations like this:

Example:

You:	I think it must be an adjective.
Partner:	Yes, and I think it describes the weather.
You:	I think it might be 'lovely' or 'beautiful'.
Partner:	Yes, or it could be 'sunny' or 'fine'.

3 Read this newspaper article quickly to understand the general sense. Ignore the words you do not know.

Are these statements about the article true or false?

1 A man arrived in Brampton covered in blood.
2 The blood may be human or animal.
3 Nobody is missing from the area.
4 The man may have killed somebody.
5 The police are looking for his jacket and trousers.

4 Read again more carefully and choose the correct alternatives for these words in the text.

1 *snowbound* (line 3)

is
A an adverb
B an adjective
C a noun

It means
A blocked by snow
B snowing a lot
C a thing for clearing snow

2 *chin* (line 4)

is
A a noun
B a verb
C an adjective

It means
A a part of the body
B a piece of clothing
C a type of knife

3 *frogmen* (line 12)

is
A a verb
B a noun
C an adjective

It means
A an animal
B sub-aqua divers
C a way of swimming

4 *sheds* (line 14)

is
A a verb
B a noun
C an adverb

It means
A tools and equipment
B digging holes
C small wooden buildings

Gory riddle of 'wolfman'

by Graham Bell

IT has all the ingredients of what Sherlock Holmes would call "a three-pipe problem."

Out of the snowbound lanes walked a man, covered in blood from his chin to his knees, who announced to police: "I am a werewolf."

At first detectives thought the fresh blood caking his faded cream jacket belonged to an animal. But tests established it as human. Yesterday, with the man refusing to reveal any information, officers were trying to account for all 6,000 residents of Brampton, near Carlisle, Cumbria.

Frogmen scoured lakes and the River Irthing which runs past the market town. Gardeners checked their sheds and families rang round sons, daughters, cousins and aunts.

So whose blood is it? "If only we knew," said James Shaw, owner of the Sands House Hotel, from whose car park the "werewolf" was picked up last Tuesday. "The police are being very thorough and are checking every man, woman and child. They have been back to us five times."

The man, who lives near Brampton, has been questioned, but gives vague, enigmatic answers. Search parties have re-traced every footstep he is known to have made. Tracker dogs have combed woods and fields and people who spotted the strange, dishevelled figure have been interviewed at length.

Detective Chief Superintendent Stephen Reed said yesterday: "We are either looking for a body or someone who is seriously injured. The amount of blood is consistent with one or the other. It is like a jigsaw puzzle you start from the wrong end. We have the centre piece and are now looking for bits to complete the picture."

Yesterday 30 uniformed officers and 12 detectives were cross-checking electoral rolls and picking their way over frozen fields near Hadrian's Wall. They are still searching for a black leather jacket which the man is believed to have discarded before his dramatic entrance into Brampton.

On Friday a man was remanded in custody by Carlisle magistrates charged with burglary and assaulting a police officer.

5 Now complete the following table for the words shown below from the text.

Word	Line	Type of Word	Meaning in Text
knees	4	noun (plural)	joints half-way down leg

faded (7)	footstep (24)	dishevelled (27)
scoured (12)	tracker (25)	jigsaw (33)
enigmatic (23)	combed (25)	rolls (37)
retraced (24)	spotted (26)	discarded (40)

Check your answers with your partner by practising as in exercise 2 on page 53.

READING

Read the article again more carefully to answer these multiple-choice questions.

1 The man who walked into Brampton said
- A nothing that was helpful to the police.
- B that he had killed someone in the town.
- C that the blood was from a wolf.
- D that someone was seriously injured.

2 What have the police been trying to do?
- A Follow the man around Brampton.
- B Find out where the man lives.
- C Discover where the blood came from.
- D Make sure the blood is human and not animal.

3 What do the police think?
- A Someone could have been murdered.
- B Someone must have been killed.
- C Someone might have tried to kill the man.
- D The man may have been attacked by a wolf.

What do you think is the explanation for this mystery?

GRAMMAR GR p179
Relative Clauses

1 What is a **werewolf**?

1 A person who changes into a wild animal.
2 An animal which looks like a man.
3 A place where a murder is committed.

2 For each of these words from the passage, write a definition using *who*, *which* or *where*.

1 detectives (line 6)
2 residents (10)
3 frogmen (12)
4 sheds (14)
5 search parties (24)
6 tracker dogs (25)

3 What is the difference between these two sentences?

The man, who lives near Brampton, has been questioned.
People who spotted the man have been interviewed.

Punctuate these sentences to show whether they contain defining or non-defining clauses.

1 Sherlock Holmes who lived in London was a famous detective.
2 The leather jacket which the man was wearing has not been found.
3 Brampton which is a small town is near Carlisle in the north of England.
4 The man who walked into Brampton was covered in blood.

HELP WITH VOCABULARY

Phrasal Verbs

In the Use of English paper you are sometimes asked to complete sentences using phrasal verbs. You may have to add a preposition to a verb.

Example: He gets up at eight o'clock every morning.

or you may have to add a verb to a preposition.

Example: He *got* off the bus when it reached the bus station.

1 With your partner discuss the following:

1 How is a phrasal verb different to other verbs?
2 How can you tell a phrasal verb from a simple verb + preposition?
3 In what sort of language are phrasal verbs most common?

2 Decide which of the following are phrasal verbs and which are not.

Example: I *get up* at eight o'clock. = phrasal verb (meaning 'rise from bed')
I *go to* work by bus. = verb + preposition

1 I *came to* school late this morning.
2 I *came across* this book of yours in my room.
3 As soon as he arrived in Athens, he went to the hotel and *checked in*.
4 I'd like to *send* this letter *to* Spain, please.
5 A large crowd was there to *see* him *off* at the airport.
6 I *slept in* the guest bedroom last night.
7 He *lives in* a ground-floor flat.
8 After lunch, he *set off* in the direction of the city centre.
9 These old buildings are going to be *pulled down*.
10 He *works at* the local hospital.

3 Add a preposition to each of these sentences to complete the expression formed from TURN.

Example: Although he wasn't looking forward to the party, it turned out to be very enjoyable.

1 I can't hear the television, do you mind if I turn the volume ________?
2 Soon after leaving, the tourists were forced to turn ________ because of bad weather.
3 When she kissed the frog, it turned ________ a prince.
4 An uncle she hadn't heard from for 10 years suddenly turned ________ at her home last night.
5 Nigel's disappointed because his request for a salary increase has been turned ________.

Now match one of the verbs in the box to each of the phrasal verbs in exercise 3.

increase	appear	return
refuse	change	

LISTENING 3

You will hear a lawyer talking about what happened to the burglar who broke into a house and stole some jewellery.

1 Put a preposition in each space.

1 She was found guilty ________ theft.
2 A woman was seen leaving the house ________ a large bag.
3 She was arrested ________ the police.
4 The police went to her flat and found her ________ possession of the jewels.
5 Some jewellery was stolen ________ the house in Brighton.
6 In court she was accused ________ stealing the jewels.
7 She was sentenced ________ two years in prison.
8 The police provided evidence ________ her guilt.
9 The police charged her ________ stealing the jewellery.
10 She was released ________ bail.

Listen to check and put the sentences in the correct order.

2 Look at these phrases from the listening text.

Someone broke into her house.
The burglar got in through a back door.
Then walked out through the front door.
A neighbour was looking out of her window.
The police looked into the details.
They got the case ready.

1 There are four phrasal verbs in the phrases above. Can you identify them?

2 Match one of the following verbs to each of the phrasal verbs you have found.

entered by force
prepared
investigated
entered

3 Replace the word in brackets in each of the following sentences with the correct form of a phrasal verb from the box below.

Example: He (requested) a glass of water. *asked for*

1 Can you (return) that pen I lent you? ________
2 I was (raised) on a farm. ________
3 We (visited) my aunt on the way home. ________
4 The match has been (cancelled). ________
5 That music will never (become popular). ________
6 The cake was (divided) into four pieces. ________
7 I have to (stop) eating sweets. ________
8 Can you (wait) a moment, please? ________
9 The train was (delayed) for two hours.
10 ________ (Select) the one you like best. ________

give back	cut up	pick out	call off
give up	~~ask for~~	catch on	call on
bring up	hang on	hold up	

REVISION TEST 4

1 Fill each of the blanks with one suitable word which completes the word or expression formed from BREAK.

Example: Don't leave your car radio aerial extended in case someone breaks it off.

1 Someone broke ________ the school last night.
2 A number of prisoners have broken ________ of the local prison.
3 The police broke ________ the fight between the rival gangs.
4 To get into the house they had to break ________ the door.
5 The police car stopped to help a driver whose van had broken ________.

2 You will hear Paul talking about a break-in at his flat.

Look at these pictures. For each of the articles indicated, put a tick (✓) in the box if they have been stolen or damaged.

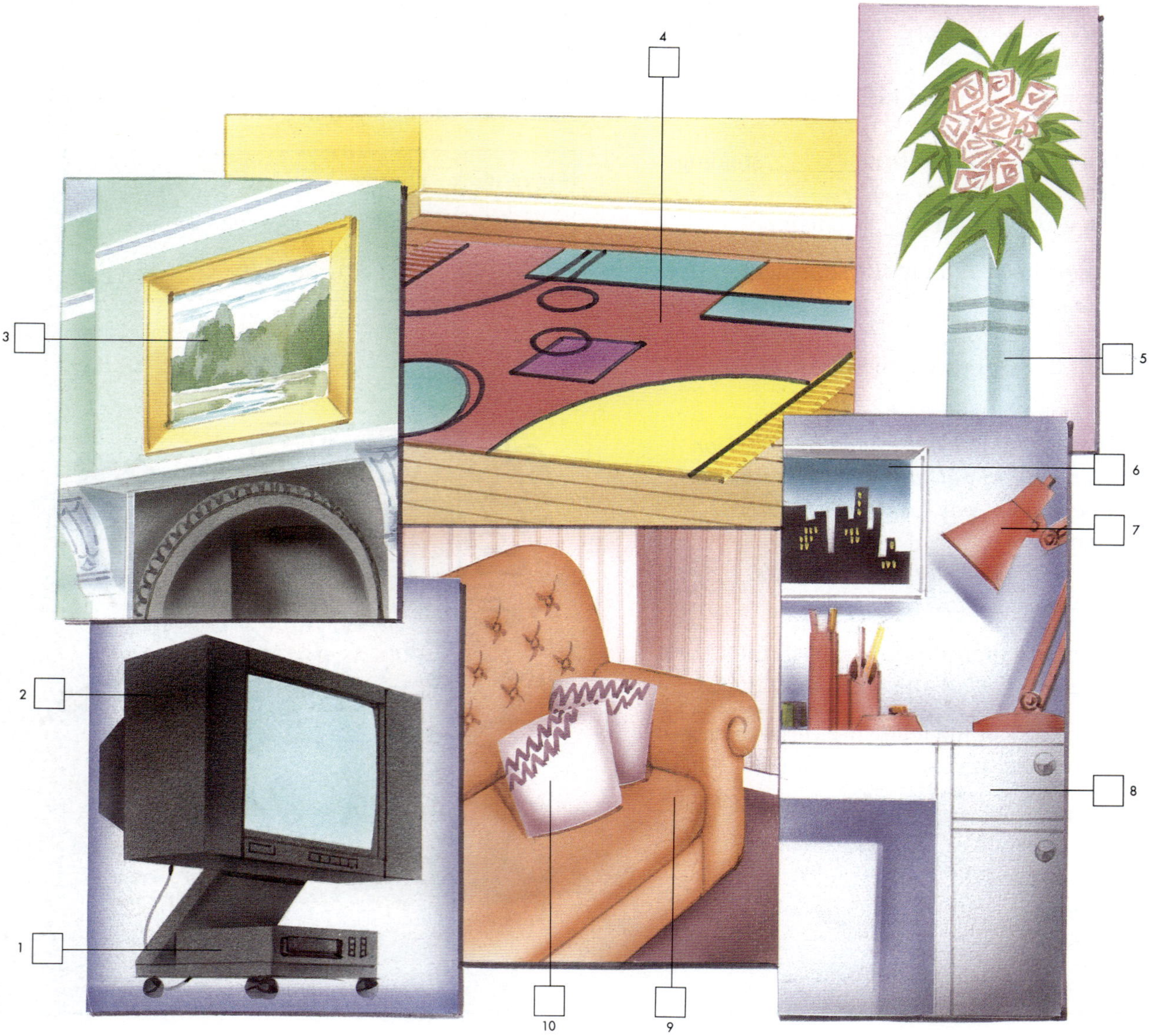

3 Choose from these compositions.

1 What are some good ways of protecting your home against burglars? What are the disadvantages of these methods?
2 You were recently a witness to an armed robbery. Write a letter to a friend explaining what happened.
3 What can be said for and against longer terms of imprisonment to deter young offenders?

4 Read the passage and then finish the sentences or answer the questions by choosing the best alternative.

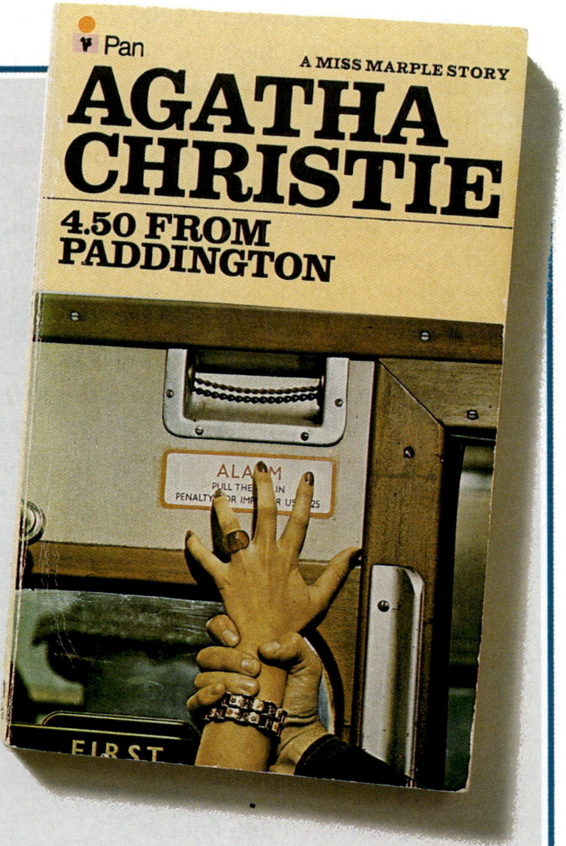

The train clattered over points and passed through a station.

Then it began suddenly to slow down, presumably in obedience to a signal. For some minutes it crawled along, then stopped; presently it began to move forward again. Another up-train passed them, though with less vehemence than the first one. The train gathered speed again. At that moment another train, also on a down-line, swerved inwards towards them, for a moment with almost alarming effect. For a time the two trains ran parallel, now one gaining a little, now the other. Mrs McGillicuddy looked from her window through the windows of the parallel carriages. Most of the blinds were down, but occasionally the occupants of the carriages were visible. The other train was not very full and there were many empty carriages.

At the moment when the two trains gave the illusion of being stationary, a blind in one of the carriages flew up with a snap. Mrs McGillicuddy looked into the lighted first-class carriage that was only a few feet away.

Then she drew her breath in with a gasp and half-rose to her feet.

Standing with his back to the window and to her was a man. His hands were round the throat of a woman who faced him, and he was slowly, remorselessly, strangling her. Her eyes were starting from their sockets, her face was purple and congested. As Mrs McGillicuddy watched, fascinated, the end came; the body went limp and crumpled in the man's hands.

At the same moment, Mrs McGillicuddy's train slowed down again and the other began to gain speed. It passed forward and a moment or two later it had vanished from sight.

Almost automatically Mrs McGillicuddy's hand went up to the communication cord, then paused, irresolute. After all, what use would it be ringing the cord of the train in which she was travelling? The horror of what she had seen at such close quarters, and the unusual circumstances, made her feel paralysed. Some immediate action was necessary — but what?

The door of her compartment was drawn back and a ticket collector said, 'Ticket, please.'

1 Mrs McGillicuddy's train was travelling
- A very fast.
- B at a constant speed.
- C at varying speeds.
- D very slowly.

2 Mrs McGillicuddy's train and the train where the murder took place
- A were travelling in the same direction at the same speed.
- B were both waiting at a station.
- C were travelling in opposite directions but very slowly.
- D were both stationary because of some signals.

3 What did Mrs McGillicuddy think?
- A The woman had been murdered.
- B The woman may have survived.
- C She feared that the murderer had seen her.
- D She hoped that she had saved the woman's life.

4 Why didn't Mrs McGillicuddy pull the cord?
- A She was too frightened by what she had seen.
- B She preferred to tell the ticket inspector.
- C She didn't think it would help the situation.
- D Her train was slowing down in any case.

5 Mr and Mrs Compton would like to move house. Below are some details about the Compton family, and some descriptions of houses in their area. Using the information given complete the two paragraphs below in your own words.

Mr and Mrs Compton
3 children (1 working, 2 at school)
elderly grandmother
husband commutes to work by train, doesn't like DIY
wife is a translator – needs an office at home, also a keen gardener
2 cars

1 I think the family should choose _______ because _______

2 They certainly shouldn't choose _______ because _______

28 Malling Hill

This unusual terraced house has five bedrooms on four separate floors + living room, kitchen, 2 bathrooms and a basement storage area. The house is on a steep hill about 15 minutes walk from the station and is close to local schools. It is in perfect condition throughout and there is a large back garden.

106 Anderson Road

A big family will enjoy this well-maintained semi-detached house about 1 mile from the station and handy for the city centre, schools and local shops. The house has 6 bedrooms and 2 bathrooms as well as a large living room and kitchen. There are small front and back gardens (some work needed), and a double garage.

14 Castle Crescent

Just 5 minutes from the station, this house is also convenient for schools and the city centre. The house contains 5 bedrooms, 1 bathroom, a modern kitchen and living room. It has a single garage and the enormous garden contains a heated shed with large windows. The house requires some redecoration work.

UNIT 5 PLAY TO WIN

VOCABULARY

①

③

②

④

1

1 Name the sport or game in each picture, and say:
What equipment is necessary.
What the aim is.
What skills are necessary.

2 What is the difference between a sport and a game?

3 Divide these activities into three groups:
A Sports.
B Games.
C Activities which are both sports and games.

squash	tennis	Scrabble
billiards	fishing	hockey
Trivial Pursuits	rollerskating	skiing
basketball	parachuting	chess
swimming	golf	rugby

2 Sports Quiz

In groups of three decide which are the correct answers to these questions.

1 Which of these sports is not played with a racket?

A squash
B badminton
C tennis
D cricket

2 Which of these sports uses an oval ball?

A soccer
B rugby
C water polo
D hockey

3 Which of these sports is not played over a net?

A volleyball
B tennis
C squash
D badminton

4 Which of these sports does not involve throwing something?

A javelin
B shotput
C pole vault
D discus

5 Which of these is not a swimming style?

A butterfly
B crawl
C breaststroke
D diving

6 Which of these is not a winter sport?

A tobogganing
B skating
C jogging
D skiing

7 Which of these is not an Olympic games sport?

A parachuting
B rowing
C shooting
D archery

8 Where was the 1990 World Cup final held?

A Rome
B Milan
C Naples
D Turin

9 Which of these is not a martial art?

A judo
B karate
C croquet
D jujitsu

10 Which of these games is not played on a table?

A snooker
B dominoes
C darts
D billiards

11 Which of these is not a water sport?

A windsurfing
B abseiling
C rowing
D snorkelling

12 Which of these games does not use goals?

A ice-hockey
B polo
C baseball
D lacrosse

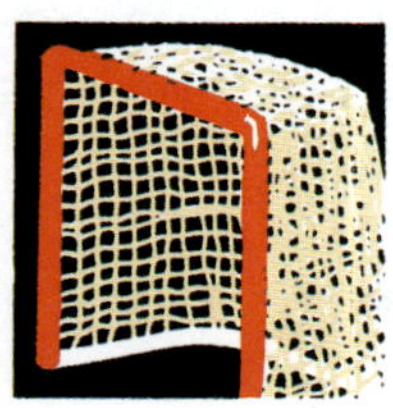

GRAMMAR GR p180

Time Linkers

1 Here are some facts about the game of Scrabble.

'Scrabble' is a trade mark of JW Spear & Sons plc

Imagine that either you are playing the game of Scrabble for the first time, or, if you know Scrabble, you have to explain the rules to a friend.

Decide which of these sentences contain important facts about how to play the game.

Scrabble can be played by two to four players.
The board can be folded for storage.
The first word must cover the star.
Scrabble is played using small tiles
Scrabble is useful to practise spelling.
Each tile has a number to indicate its value for scoring.
You need a pencil and paper to keep the score.
Each player must take seven tiles from the bag.
The game was invented by an American.
Covering the coloured squares on the board gives extra points.
Scrabble can be played at any time of day.
On each tile there is a letter of the alphabet.
The game ends when the bag is empty and one player has used all his or her tiles.
Each new word must use at least one letter from a word already on the board.
As letters are used they must be replaced from the bag.
Scrabble is not expensive to buy.
Scrabble is very popular in the USA.
Small Scrabble sets can be bought to use when travelling.

Compare with your partner.

2 [...] the instructions below fill each of the numbered blanks with one of the expressions from the box. Use each word or phrase once only.

during	as soon as	firstly	or	until	after that
then	to begin with	while	so that	either	lastly

(1) *To begin with* you need a Scrabble board, a set of letters and a pencil and paper to keep the score. You can play with two, three or four players.

(2) _______ each person takes one tile from the bag, and the person with the highest number on his or her tile will start the game. (3) _______ each person takes six more tiles from the bag so that everyone has seven letters.

The first player starts by making a word which covers the star in the centre of the board. (4) _______ the next player makes another word by (5) _______ creating a new word which crosses the original word (6) _______ by adding more letters to the original word.

(7) _______ players make a word they must take more letters from the bag (8) _______ they always have seven. All the players continue making words in this way (9) _______ there are no more letters in the bag and one person has used all their tiles.

(10) _______ playing try to cover the coloured squares as these increase the number of points on the tile. (11) _______ the game one person keeps the score by adding up all the numbers in each word played.

(12) _______ it should be remembered that Scrabble can take a very long time if the players are really keen and, of course, players get better with practice.

WRITING

1 Think of a game or sport you know well. Make a list of the important facts or instructions you need to know in order to play the game.
2 Make sure your points are in a logical order.
3 Use your list to write some instructions for the game, using the passage above as an example.

LISTENING 1

1 Before you listen look at the list of sports below.

1 What do they all have in common?
2 Divide them into two groups, A and B, and give each group a title.

hockey	squash	baseball
rugby	badminton	tennis
American football	soccer	golf
volleyball	cricket	polo
table tennis	basketball	billiards

3 Now divide the same words into three groups X, Y and Z and give each group a title.
4 Compare with other students. Did you make the same or different groups?
5 Listen to this radio interview and write down all the names of sports which you hear mentioned.

2 Now listen again and choose the best alternative A, B, C or D.

1 We know that the ancient Egyptians played ball games because
A it is mentioned in ancient stories.
B ancient works of art show them.
C sports equipment was found in tombs.
D people have always said so.

A	
B	
C	
D	

2 When were racquets invented?
A In the eleventh century.
B In the fifteenth century.
C In the sixteenth century.
D In the nineteenth century.

A	
B	
C	
D	

3 Before the nineteenth century
A the games had no rules at all.
B the rules were different in different places.
C nobody followed the rules.
D people couldn't afford to follow rules.

A	
B	
C	
D	

4 In the nineteenth century
A many new games were invented.
B many old games were rediscovered.
C the old games were organised more formally.
D new games developed out of the old games.

A	
B	
C	
D	

GRAMMAR GR p180

Used to

1 Look at these phrases from the listening text.

Each town or district ***used to have*** *its own version of the same basic game.*

People ***used to work out*** *the rules over the years.*

1 When did these things happen?
2 Did they happen at one specific point in time?
3 Do they happen now?

Look at these examples:

Our football team *used to wear* blue shirts.

Do they wear blue shirts now?	(No)
Did they wear them often?	(Yes)
When did they wear them?	(In the past)

American football *didn't use to be* so popular.

Is it popular now?	(Yes)
Was it popular in the past?	(No)

Did you use to play table tennis at your old school?

N.B *Used to* does not exist in the present. The present of *used to* is *usually*.

2 Put the correct form of the verb (present, past or *used to* + infinitive) in these sentences.

1 When I was at school we *used to play* hockey twice a week. (play)
2 I ________ to the gym three times a week now that I have a car. (go)
3 Skiing ________ a sport for rich people only but now many people can take part. (be)
4 I only ________ skiing twice during my holiday in Switzerland. (go)
5 My father ________ me to see football matches on Saturday afternoons before I was old enough to go alone. (take)
6 He ________ but when he realised it affected his game he gave up. (smoke)
7 I ________ tennis and golf regularly when the weather is good. (play)
8 Before our local pool was built I ________ six kilometres by bicycle to do my training. (travel)

3 Discuss these questions:

1 What sports do you play now? How often do you play?
2 What sports did you use to play?
3 Why did you give them up?
4 How has sport changed in recent years?

Talk about:		
	equipment	facilities in your area
	clothes	popularity
	number of spectators	sport on television

LISTENING 2

Alice and Barry are talking about learning to ski. Listen and tick (✓) the problems which Barry had when he went skiing for the first time.

- ☐ expensive equipment
- ☐ too much snow
- ☐ too many people
- ☐ risk of accidents
- ☐ transport problems
- ☐ bad weather
- ☐ language difficulties
- ☐ bad teachers
- ☐ cost of lessons
- ☐ aches and pains

GRAMMAR *GR p180*

Past Perfect

1 Look at these phrases from the listening text.

I'd never tried it before
They'd already had lots of practice
I'd never felt so miserable in my life

1 Which tense is used?
2 Why?

Barry uses the Past Perfect tense to talk about things that happened before the story, which he is telling in the Past Simple tense.

When we tell a story, we set a time in the past in which the narrative takes place. When we refer to times and periods before that, we indicate this by using the Past Perfect.

Look at these examples:

	Tense	Time
I woke up early on Saturday morning	Past Simple	Saturday
It had been a very tiring week	Past Perfect	the week before Saturday
I'd never felt so tired	Past Perfect	in my life until then

Compare:

	Tense	Time
I arrived there late on Friday evening	Past Simple	Friday pm
It had been a very tiring journey	Past Perfect	before I arrived
I went to bed and fell asleep immediately	Past Simple	after I arrived

2 Put the correct tense (Past Simple or Past Perfect) in each of these sentences.

1 I arrived late at the stadium and the match ________. (start)
2 My legs ached after the match. I ________ tennis for over five years. (play)
3 The team had a good season in 1992. They ________ nearly all their matches. (win)
4 Before the Olympic games few people ________ of synchronised swimming. (hear)
5 We invited Geoff to our party but he ________ to go away that weekend. (arrange)
6 She started playing golf at the age of ten and soon ________ a regular player at the local club. (become)
7 John looked at the water below him and froze. He ________ from the top board before. (never dive)
8 As she ________ in a car rally before she was able to give him some good advice. (take part)

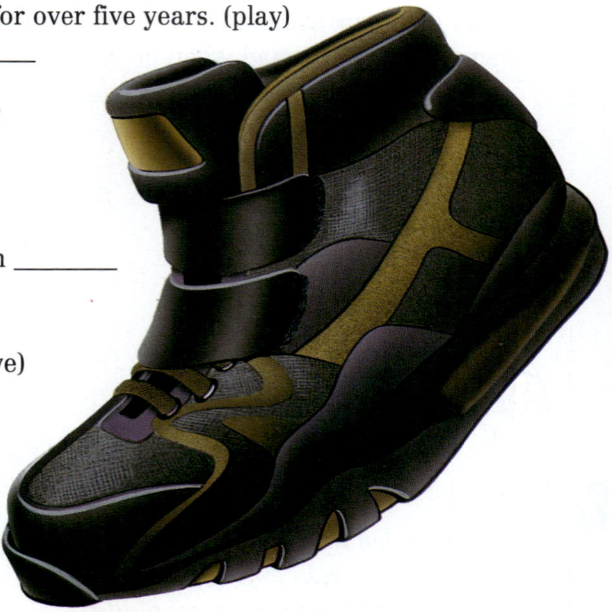

READING

1 Discuss:

How important is it to have the right clothes and equipment when you play a sport?

Are there fashions in sports clothes in your country?

Do you think it is important to wear clothes with 'designer' labels?

2 Read this article from a TV magazine about the TV programme 'Family Matters' and decide whether these statements are true or false. Ignore any words you do not understand.

1 The fashion for expensive designer trainers came to Britain from America.
2 Kelly's father is unemployed.
3 Kelly liked the trainers her mother bought her.
4 Kelly's classmates had always been nice to her before she started wearing the trainers.
5 In Kelly's old school the children hadn't been forced to wear their school uniform.

FASHION'S VICTIM

Teenage trainer mania has swept America, with reports of children being mugged and even murdered for their fashionable and expensive footwear. As this week's Family Matters discovers, this obsession with designer labels has reached Britain. Recently a girl was slashed in the face because she wouldn't 'give' another child her trendy new jacket.

But not having the right gear can also make children targets, like 14-year-old Kelly Parslow, from Birmingham. Her parents can't afford to buy her the 'in' clothes, such as Reebok or Nike trainers and shell suits (her father is on indefinite sick leave and her mother, Lynn, has two younger children as well). Last summer her mother did buy her some trainers, not a fashionable make, but ones which loked similar and cost only £7.99.

Kelly was happy with them, but when she wore them to school, her classmates weren't. 'They all started taking the mickey straight away,' she recalls. 'They said "How much did those things cost?", and they pushed me, called me a pauper and made up songs about them. Then, after school, a group of seven or eight girls lay in wait for her, and scratched and kicked her so badly that she ended up in casualty suffering from shock and contusions to her spine.

Her mother Lynn Parslow says: 'In my day, if you'd got the gear, you felt sorry for the ones who hadn't. You certainly didn't taunt them.' Kelly had been picked on before, because she was quiet, hardworking and not interested in fashion — but not like this. She now goes to another school where the uniform rules are strictly observed. 'It's much nicer there,' says Kelly. 'Nobody minds about fashion. There are a lot of other children in my position, who can't afford things, and everyone leaves them alone.'

3 Unknown Words

Try to guess the meaning of these words underlined in the text. Add to the list any other words which you do not know.

Word	Line	Type of word	Possible meaning
mania	(1)	noun	an obsession
swept	(1)	past participle	
slashed	(5)		
trendy	(6)		
gear	(7)		
targets	(7)		
taking the mickey	(15)		
recalls	(16)		
pauper	(17)		
scratched	(19)		
taunt	(22)		
picked on	(23)		

WRITING

The Narrative Composition

1 Look at the five pictures here and on the following page. With your partner decide the best order for the pictures to make a story.

2 Read this account of the day. Is the story similar or different to yours? What about the order of the pictures?

A few years ago on a skiing holiday in the Dolomites I had one of the worst experiences of my life.

My friend and I had decided not to ski that day, the sun was shining and the snow was melting fast. We had decided, **instead,** to take the ski-lift to the top of the mountain and have a walk around, taking our picnic lunch with us.

As there was little snow left we met very few skiers and the bar at the top of the lift was empty. **After drinking** a quick cup of coffee we set out to explore the mountain top. We had lunch, sitting on a rock overlooking a deep wooded ravine. After finishing our sandwiches we decided to walk a little way further **before turning back** and following the path back to the bar.

The weather changed quite suddenly. We had been too busy talking to notice the approaching black clouds, but suddenly the sun disappeared and it became quite cold. We decided to turn back immediately and before long, reached our lunch spot. **To our horror, however,** we noticed that two paths led away from the spot through the trees. We hadn't noticed this before, and realised that we didn't know which path to take. **Although** we had a map with us, it wasn't helpful as it only showed one path through the woods. **To make matters worse,** it began to snow and we realised that soon we might not be able to find the path at all.

3 What do you think will happen next? With your partner discuss some possible endings to the story.

Read the end of the story on page 71. Is it the same as your story or different?

Despite all this, neither of us panicked and, **after a brief discussion,** we decided to choose the right-hand path. After about an hour of walking we realised that we hadn't recognised a single landmark and that the snow was falling faster and faster. What should we do? Should we turn back? It would take an hour just to reach the lunch spot. We would never get back to the ski-lift **before it closed** at 5.00 pm. There was no alternative but to carry on or to face a night on the mountain!

I was just beginning to get really frightened **when** I heard a shout in the distance. We stopped and, **after a moment's silence,** began to shout at the tops of our voices. We turned a corner of the path and saw ahead of us the ski-lift station. We had made it! **However,** it was not the top of the slope, but the bottom. **Without realising it** we had walked all the way down the mountain side.

Afterwards, in the safety of the hotel, I realised how lucky we had been and how close to disaster we had come.

4 The complete story is divided into five paragraphs, plus an introduction and conclusion.

1 How do we recognise a paragraph?

2 How did the writer know when to end one paragraph and begin another?

3 Can you give each paragraph a title?

4 What information is included in the introduction and conclusion?

5

1 Which tense is used for most of the story?

2 Which other tenses are used?

3 Read the story again. Underline the sentences in which other tenses are used and decide why. Compare with your partner.

6 Look at the words and phrases in bold type.

1 What contribution do they make to the composition?

2 Look at these phrases:
- A After that we went home.
- B After drinking our coffee we went home.
- C After coffee we went home.
- D Afterwards we went home.
- E After I had finished my coffee I went home.

What are the rules for using *after*?

3 Try writing some more phrases using *before*. Are the rules the same?

7 What is the difference between *although* and *despite*?

Finish each of the sentences in such a way that it means exactly the same as the sentence printed before it.

1 Despite feeling cold we kept walking.
Although ______________________

2 Although it was sunny I felt quite cold.
Despite ______________________

3 Despite the fact that it was snowing, I felt warm.
Although ______________________

4 Despite the large amount of snow, we had our picnic.
Although ______________________

5 Although we had a map we got lost.
Despite ______________________

NB Although = Even though
Despite = In spite of

HELP WITH WRITING

Narrative composition

It is just as important to plan a narrative composition as it is to plan the type we looked at in Unit One. It is difficult to concentrate on both writing the story and inventing the story at the same time, so you should:

1 Make notes of your ideas.
2 Make a plan of your paragraphs.
3 Write your introduction.

In the exam you have to write between 120 and 180 words in your composition. If you choose to write a narrative, it will probably need to be about 180 words. The story you read on pages 70 and 71 is about twice that length, but it is a useful model of how to organise your writing.

To begin with, you might find it easier to write a longer story without a limit of words, and later to practise writing shorter stories within a time limit (45 minutes for each composition) as exam practice.

Choose one of the following titles for your composition:

1 Write a story about one of the happiest days of your life.
2 Write a story about a day when everything went wrong.
3 Write a story which begins 'It was an experience I will never forget'.

Make a list of the events in the narrative, and decide where you will divide the paragraphs. Don't forget that you will have a separate introduction and conclusion.

paragraph	model composition	your composition
1	1 decided not to ski 2 went up ski-lift	
2	3 long walk 4 lunch 5 walked a bit further	
3	6 weather changed 7 turned back 8 two paths	
4	9 long walk in snow – fear	
5	10 home at last	

Now write your introduction. It should set the scene and the time.

You are now ready to write the paragraphs of your composition. Remember to use *after, before, although* and *despite*.

REVISION TEST 5

1 Finish each of the following sentences in such a way that it means exactly the same as the sentence printed before it.

Example: I haven't laughed so much for ages.
It's ages *since I laughed so much*.

1 Originally, tennis was an indoor game.
Tennis used ______________________________

2 I haven't worn a tracksuit for years.
It's ______________________________

3 Hang-gliding is not as frightening as free-fall parachuting.
Free-fall parachuting ______________________________

4 Let's go skiing next weekend.
Why ______________________________

5 The sports shop is repairing my tennis racquet at the moment.
I am ______________________________

6 I haven't played this game before.
It's the first ______________________________

7 Although it was raining, they played tennis.
Despite ______________________________

8 They finished their tea and then they left.
After ______________________________

9 When you are going mountain climbing, you should check the weather forecast first.
Before ______________________________

10 Despite his injury, he continued to play.
Although ______________________________

2 For each question 1–10 you must choose the word or phrase which best completes the sentence.

1 Skis used to be made ________ wood.
A of **B** out **C** by **D** for

2 The referee's job is to make sure the ________ of the game are observed.
A laws **B** regulations **C** norms **D** rules

3 He walked up to the rostrum with a smile. It was the sixth time he ________ a gold medal.
A has won **B** won **C** had won **D** was winning

4 The length of the match depends ________ the age of the players.
A on **B** from **C** by **D** to

5 Some sportsmen and women insist that ________ part is more important than winning.
A taken **B** take **C** to take **D** taking

6 Before ________ the changing rooms, make sure you have all your valuables with you.
A to leave **B** leaving **C** having left **D** leave

7 At the end of the match he was ________ with a trophy and a bottle of champagne.
A presented **B** given **C** prized **D** donated

8 Due to bad weather, the match has been put ________ until next Wednesday.
A forward **B** off **C** out **D** ahead

9 I haven't played hockey ________ ages.
A from **B** since **C** during **D** for

10 Without ________ it, he had overtaken most of the other competitors.
A realising **B** realised **C** realise **D** to realise

3 Complete each of the following sentences with one or two words to form an expression with LOOK.

Example: Ask someone to look *after* your money and valuables while you go swimming.

1 We are looking ________ young people who would like to join a new tennis club.
2 As it was a new sport, we couldn't look ________ the rules in a book.
3 The football association is looking ________ reports of corruption.
4 Mr Brown, the team manager, was a person all the players could look ________ ________.
5 Look ________! You're going to ski into a tree if you're not careful.

4 Fill each of the numbered blanks in the following passage. Use only one word in each space.

Skiing was originally invented because people in some areas ________ (1) to cross country which was ________ (2) covered with a lot of snow for large parts of the year.

We know that men and women have been skiing for at ________ (3) 4000 years. The remains of ancient skis have been ________ (4) from that period as ________ (5) as good examples of rock carvings showing early skiers. Old documents describe how people ________ (6) skis to follow animals, and ________ (7) type of hunting was ________ (8) until the sixteenth century.

Today, skiing, which was originally ________ (9) a means of transport, has developed ________ (10) a leisure activity and an important part of the tourist ________ (11) in some countries. It is now enjoyed ________ (12) an increasing number of people each year.

5 Choose one of the following compositions. Your answer must be of between 120 and 180 words.

1 Write the story of a great sporting achievement.
2 Write a story beginning with the phrase, 'Finally the great day had arrived ...'.
3 How is your life today different from that of people of your parents' or grandparents' generation?

UNIT 6 RETURN TICKET

SPEAKING

1 Look at the picture. With your partner decide:

Where the people are.
Why they are travelling.
How they feel.

2 Read these three passages. Decide which passage best describes the picture.

1 **The journey seemed to go on for ever and they soon tired of looking out of the window. Rosie eventually got into conversation with the young couple opposite and this soon degenerated into a joke-telling session that, in the end, came to involve the whole carriage. This had the advantage of taking their minds off the length of the journey.**

2 **Sitting in the departure lounge was an adventure in itself. The airport authorities, knowing by bitter experience how fractious delayed passengers could become, had provided a whole range of pre-flight entertainment. There were clowns for the children, an impromptu fashion show for the adults and free magazines for all those who wanted to sit quietly in a corner.**

3 **There was nowhere to sit, and everyone hung about aimlessly, eyes fixed to the indicator board, vaguely hoping that the next clattering change to the information would be good news for them. Inevitably, what they saw were more delays and cancellations.**

3 Imagine you are going on a long air, rail or road journey with your family, or with friends. What things would you take with you to make the time pass more quickly?

Make a list and then compare with your partner.

What are the advantages and disadvantages of the things on your list?

Are some more suitable for journeys by car, plane or train?

READING

1 Read this newspaper article and for each of the questions choose the best answer, A, B, C or D.

FURY ON THE 22

You can imagine how frustrated Tracy Lewis (24) of Linton felt after a seventy-five-minute wait for the delayed number 22 bus last Monday morning. Her frustration turned to anger, however, when she offered the driver a ten-pound note for her three-pound return fare to the city centre. 'Sorry,' he said, 'I'm not allowed to give change.'

The new rule, which came into force last week, means that passengers will have to have the correct money or buy a ticket before boarding the bus.

'I was furious,' said Tracy, 'none of the other passengers had change because they'd all been caught out in the same way. The bus company should have let us know about this in advance.'

Tracy, in desperation, eventually gave the bus driver the ten-pound note, even though she got no change. 'I can't afford to do this every day!' she commented, 'but I have to go to work.'

The local bus company has now apologised for not giving due notice of the new policy but a spokesperson said: 'It's only like a vending machine - you just have to make sure you have the right money before you leave home. It should make it much easier for the buses to run on time if the drivers don't have to worry about giving change.'

1 Why was Tracy angry?
- A She paid more than the usual fare.
- B The fares had been increased without notice.
- C The bus was even later than usual.
- D None of the other passengers would help.

2 Why did the bus company apologise?
- A For not giving Tracy her change.
- B For the late running of the bus.
- C For not giving adequate notice.
- D For the attitude of the driver.

3 According to the bus company
- A Tracy should get her ticket from a machine.
- B people who argue make the buses late.
- C the new policy will improve punctuality.
- D you should buy a ticket before you board the bus.

GRAMMAR GR p181

Compound Adjectives

Look at these phrases from the article.

after a seventy-five-minute wait
(seventy-five-minute = adjective; wait = noun)

This means a wait of seventy-five-minutes.

a three-pound fare
(three-pound = adjective; fare = noun)

This means a fare of three pounds.

Notice that when the price or the time is used as an adjective it has no plural form.

Finish each of the following sentences in such a way that it means exactly the same as the sentence printed before it.

Example: The holiday lasted two weeks.
It was *a two-week holiday*.

1 The walk only took five minutes.
It was ______________________

2 It was a nine-month course.
The course ______________________

3 The flight lasts twenty-four hours.
It is ______________________

4 This contract is for two years.
This is ______________________

5 The car cost five thousand pounds.
It was ______________________

6 It is a three-hundred-pound holiday.
The holiday ______________________

7 The ferry crossing to the island takes two hours.
It is ______________________

8 It is a twelve-day coach tour.
The ______________________

VOCABULARY

1 **Travel Quiz**

Win the dream holiday of a lifetime!

Answer ten simple questions correctly and your name will be entered for the prize draw. First prize a four-week round-the-world trip for two with a choice of itineraries.

1. Near which city would you find Stansted Airport?
a Miami **b** London
c Melbourne **d** Edinburgh

2. Which of these islands is not in the Caribbean?
a Barbados **b** Bermuda
c Jamaica **d** Trinidad

3. Which is the capital city of Canada?
a Toronto **b** Vancouver
c Quebec **d** Ottawa

4. Which of these countries does not have dollars as the unit of currency?
a Canada **b** Australia
c New Zealand **d** Argentina

5. In which country would you find the lost city of the Incas?
a Peru **b** Ecuador
c Mexico **d** Brazil

6. Which sea separates Great Britain and Ireland?
a North Sea **b** English Channel
c Irish Sea **d** Atlantic Ocean

7. Which of these countries has the largest number of islands?
a Yugoslavia **b** Norway
c Greece **d** The Phillipines

8. Which of these countries does not have English as an official language?
a South Africa **b** Jamaica
c Iceland **d** India

9. Which is the furthest from London?
a Toronto **b** Tokyo
c Buenos Aires **d** Sydney

10. In not more than 100 words say why you think a round-the-world trip would be a good experience for you.

2 Look at these words. When they are used to talk about holidays or transport, are they usually nouns or verbs, or both?

cruise	flight	fly
trip	travel	sight-seeing
journey	crossing	

Put one of the words into the space in each of these sentences.

1 My ________ to the office each day takes me through some lovely countryside.
2 She's going to Brazil on a business ________ .
3 The ________ from Athens to New York takes more than eight hours.
4 For their honeymoon they're going on a ________around the Caribbean.
5 It has always been one of my ambitions to ________ overland to Australia.
6 We arrive in Rome at midday and after lunch there are two hours free for ________.
7 The quickest sea ________ from England to France is by hovercraft.
8 You can either take the train or you can ________ , which is quicker but more expensive.

3 Imagine you have received this telemessage.

> Congratulations!! You have won First Prize! A four-week round-the-world trip for two in February of next year. More details to follow.

1 Make a list of the countries you would most like to visit on your trip.
How would you like to travel? By air, by sea, by car, by train or on foot?
What information do you need about the countries on your list before you make your final decision?
2 Exchange ideas with a partner.

READING

1 To really enjoy a round-the-world trip you need to spend quite a long time in each place. This probably means being away from home for much longer than one month.

1 What problems do you think you would have being away from home for up to one year, for instance?
Talk to your partner about the following things:

clothes	money
health	luggage
family	accommodation

2 This article is about a couple who spent a year travelling round the world. Read it quickly and underline the parts where these things are discussed:

their route	documents
homesickness	family
health	accommodation
luggage	

3 Talk to your partner about the problems Carole and Berry had with each of the things in exercise 2.

4 Find words or expressions which mean

a escaped (para 2)
b slow and relaxing (2)
c doubts and fears (5)
d leave completely (5)
e reached crisis point (5)
f dirty and untidy (5)
g point of view (7)
h fashionable (7)
i most important (9)
j fit and healthy (12)

5 Make a note of other new words you have learned in the text which you think might be important to remember.

Road to

1 **Berry Ritchie and his wife, Carole, did it: they packed their bags, rented out their home and travelled the globe.**

2 We fled our semi-detached nest in safe, suburban, Richmond some 18 months ago. We bought round-the-world air tickets and left London early in October. Our journey took us in leisurely stages to New York and California, over the Pacific to Australia, through Hong Kong, Bali, Singapore, Thailand and Southern India and back through Europe.

3 We visited some of the most exotic places in the world and some of the least. We stayed with friends in some places, and in hotels, motels and guest houses. We travelled in taxis, buses, cars, vans, jeeps, rickshaws, trains and planes. We ate well and we ate badly. And all the time we were together. After more than twenty-five years. Just each other. Alone at last.

4 I will pass over the day that we were supposed to fly to New York and didn't because my wife lost her passport. We discovered this on the way to the airport. Several hours passed before we found it, stored for safe keeping along with her diaries in my mother's attic. It was something that could have happened to anyone.

5 At the end of the first fortnight we felt desolate. We both missed our daughter. My wife, Carole, suffered from homesickness and missed her friends and colleagues. And we were consumed with misgivings about giving up our jobs, though the desire to make a break from routine had been one of the motives behind the trip. Our feelings came to a head one morning in the rather shabby room we were renting in Brooklyn. We looked each other in the eye. 'Shall we go home?' we said together.

6 It was a rhetorical question, as we had let our house for the year and in any case the moment passed. It recurred, but with less and less intensity, though we never did stop missing our near and dear ones.

7 Less emotional and more predictable was the problem of living out of suitcases. My theory that we could buy disposable clothes as we went along was wrong, at least from the perspective of a style-conscious Englishwoman. The truth is that you get what you pay for, which in the Far East is often not much.

8 Another pressure point was accommodation. It is hard to say which is worse, a hotel room or one belonging to friends. The former lacks home comforts, the latter imposes behavioural constraints.

Freedom

9 We learned that floor space, a view and a private bathroom were vital for a stay of any length. Usually we found all three, though sometimes not before a search. We wouldn't recommend you staying in the Transit Hotel in Jakarta.

10 We didn't miss television but books were a problem, solved by begging borrowing and stealing. Books were also a major contribution to the weight of our luggage. Much of our reading was escapist, but we did discover that books about their history and culture added to our appreciation of the countries we visited.

11 We expected, of course, to be ill. Nothing serious, you understand, because we'd been inoculated against everything. But we confidently feared food poisoning, snake bites, insect stings and a variety of alien fevers. In the event I caught a cold and Carole had to have a filling replaced in Melbourne, the home of dentistry.

12 One reason for our good health was that as our journey progressed we gradually became fitter. Neither of us was in very good shape when we left home. We hadn't had time to get fit, what with all the stresses and strains of preparing to go.

13 As the days turned into weeks the people we stayed with commented on how well we looked, and how young. We felt it. We also felt something else. We felt free.

14 It couldn't last, of course. As months and continents passed, the pull of home and loved ones strengthened. Again there came a moment when we asked each other 'Shall we go home?'. This time, though, it was because we'd had enough, not because we were afraid.

15 We arrived back a year and a week after we left. After a month we recognised that being back home really had been hard!

2 Read the article more carefully to find the answers to these questions.

1 Carole lost her passport
- A in New York.
- B on the plane.
- C before the trip.
- D at the airport.

2 What prevented Carole and Berry returning home after two weeks?
- A Someone else was living in their house.
- B They had spent a lot of money on their ticket.
- C They couldn't change their planned route.
- D They didn't want to look silly.

3 Where did Carole and Berry prefer to stay?
- A In hotel rooms.
- B With friends.
- C Anywhere cheap and clean.
- D Anywhere comfortable.

4 Which books did Carole and Berry read?
- A Books they had brought with them from home.
- B Books which they bought in the countries they visited.
- C Any books they were able to find.
- D Books in many different languages.

5 Carole and Berry
- A were very healthy by the end of the trip.
- B were often ill although they had taken lots of precautions.
- C had been very healthy before leaving for the trip.
- D sometimes took precautions which made them ill.

6 Why did Carole and Berry eventually decide to go home?
- A They were homesick.
- B They were afraid.
- C A year had passed.
- D They had travelled enough.

GRAMMAR
Prepositions

1 Complete the blank in each of these sentences with one of the following prepositions.

on by in

1 I like to travel ________ train
2 I've never been ________ an inter-city train.
3 I usually go to work ________ car
4 I'll give you a lift ________ my car.

When do we use *by* and when do we use other prepositions?

2 Put a preposition in each of these sentences.

1 The fastest way from London to Glasgow is____air .
2 The cheapest way from London to Glasgow is ____ coach .
3 I'd love to go ____ a Mediterranean cruise.
4 We went to the USA ____ a jumbo jet.
5 He goes to school ____ his bike.
6 Travelling ____ train is more expensive than going ____ your car.
7 We decided not to fly ____ Ireland but to take the car ____ the ferry.
8 About sixty people can go ____ the coach. The rest will have to go ____ train.
9 If you go to the airport ____ underground you arrive ____ terminal three, but if you go ____ car you have to find the way ____ the car park ____ the terminal ____ foot.
10 The best way to reach the Scilly Isles is ____helicopter ____ Penzance, but once there you should travel ____ the main islands ____ boat.

LISTENING 1

Giving Directions

1 Joanne is new to London and has been invited to visit Dave in his flat in Walthamstow. She arrives at Walthamstow Station and can't find the way. She phones Dave. Listen to the conversation and draw the route on the map.

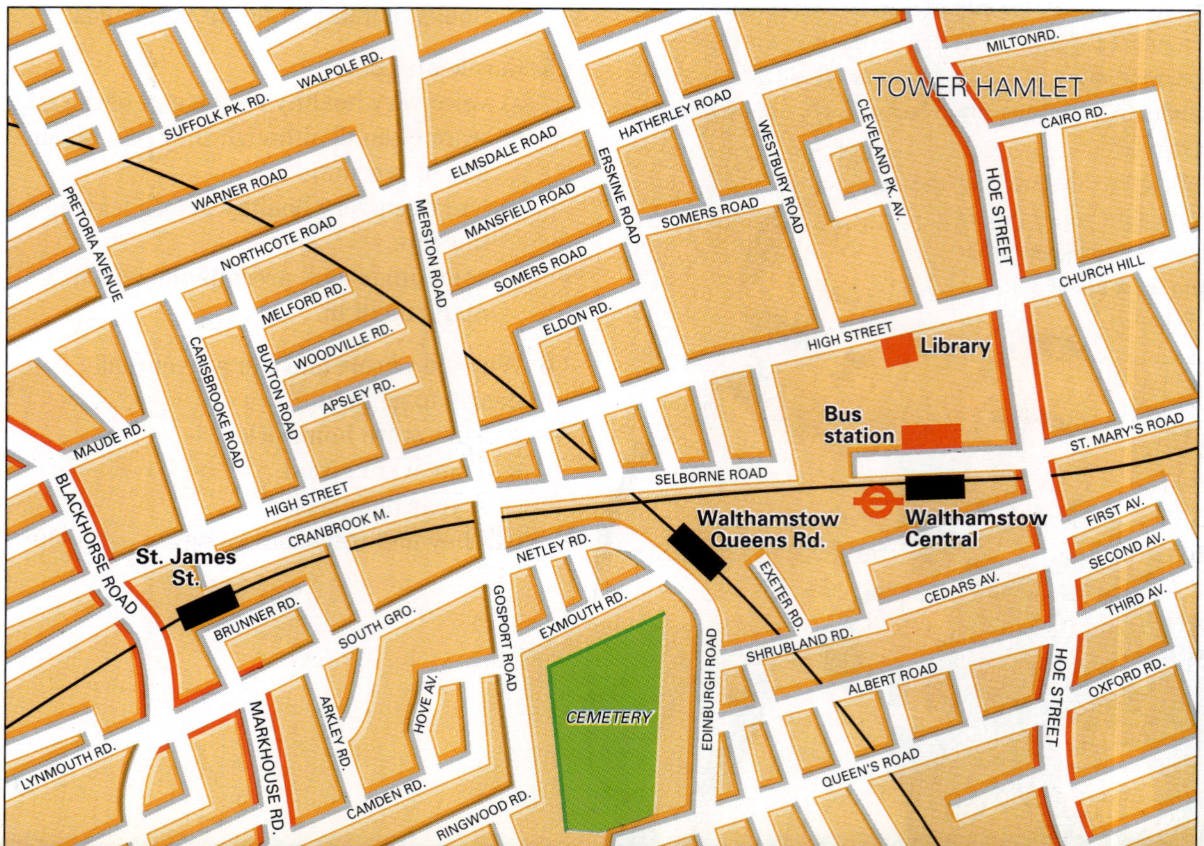

GRAMMAR
Directions

1 The language of giving directions is quite complicated and many variations are possible. To avoid making mistakes you should follow these rules:

1 Use imperatives to tell people what to do.

Examples: Turn left
Turn right
Go straight on
Walk down the road

2 Use a preposition to tell people where things are.

Examples: The bus station is on the right
It's the third turning on the left
It's opposite the station

3 Use *will* to tell people what to look for.

Examples: You will see the library on your left
You'll come to a large crossroads
You'll find my house on the right

2 Study these sentences, and say which type they are - **1, 2** or **3** above.

1 When you come to the crossroads, go straight on.
2 Turn right as you come out of the station.
3 Turn left along Main Street.
4 Walk as far as the traffic lights.
5 You'll see the Bus Station, you can't miss it.
6 It's the third turning on the right.

3 Put one preposition in each space if it is necessary.

1 Turn ____ right ____ the crossroads.
2 Walk ____ the road as far as the library.
3 Turn ____ left ____ Forest Road.
4 The shop is ____ the bus station.
5 My house is ____ Merston Road.
6 Go straight ____ at the traffic lights
7 Turn ____ left and then ____ left again.
8 It's the third house ____ the left.
9 Take the third turning ____ the left.

SPEAKING

Look again at the map of Walthamstow. Ask your partner to give you the following directions:

1 From the library to Warner Road.

2 From Walthamstow Central station to Melford Road.

WRITING

Where do people arrive in your city, town or area?
It could be at a railway station, bus station, harbour, airport or any other arrival point.

Write a letter to a friend who is coming to visit your home for the first time.

1 Apologise for not being able to meet your friend and explain why you are busy.

2 Give directions of how to get to your house from the arrival point.

LISTENING 2

You will hear Dave receive a telephone call from his friend Gianna in Italy.

As you listen make a note of the following information:

1 Gianna arrives at ________ airport on flight number ________ from ________at ________ on ________ .

2 Angelo arrives at ________ airport on flight number ________ from ________ at ________ on ________ .

3 Gianna's fax number is ________ .

GRAMMAR GR p181

Future Time 1

1 Look at these phrases from the listening text.

We arrive at different airports
Angelo arrives at Heathrow Airport

Which tense is used and why?

We use the **Present Simple** tense to refer to future time when we talk about timetables and other things which happen at fixed times and so cannot be changed.

Look at these examples:

	Tense	Time
The film begins at eight o'clock	present	tonight
The train leaves at five on Saturday morning	present	tomorrow morning
Tomorrow is her birthday	present	tomorrow

2 Look at these sentences and decide if they are right or wrong.

Examples:
My plane leaves at 18.00 (right)

(It's the same time for everybody, and I can't change it)

I meet my sister at 2 p.m. tomorrow (wrong)

(I can change the time because it only involves me and my sister)

1 Tomorrow is the first day of term.
2 I go to the theatre tomorrow.
3 Angelo starts English classes next week.
4 The party starts at 8 p.m.
5 My exam is next Monday.
6 The restaurant closes at 6 p.m.
7 I meet my friend tomorrow evening.
8 Next year is a leap year.

3 Look at the sentences which you have decided are wrong in exercise 2. Which tense can you use instead of the Present Simple to make them correct?

Example: I meet my sister at 2 p.m. (wrong)

I'm meeting my sister at 2 p.m.

I'm going to meet my sister at 2 p.m.

Both of these corrections are possible but each means something different. In each case if you ask the question *when* the answer is the same - in the future/at 2 p.m. So what is the difference?

4 Look at these sentences and decide which sentences talk about an intention and which an arrangement.

1. I'm going to do lots of shopping while I'm in Paris.
2. They're meeting Angelo at 6 p.m. outside the station.
3. He's told me he's going to study much harder next year.
4. She's travelling to Athens with Rosa.
5. I'm going to look up lots of friends during my stay.
6. We're getting a lift from a woman who lives in the same street.

5 In this letter choose the best form of the verb.

Dear Bill,

Guess what! I (1) *come/am coming/am going to come* to Toronto for a couple of days next week.

My plane (2) *arrives/is arriving/is going to arrive* in Toronto at 16.30 on Wednesday. I (3) *stay/am staying/am going to stay* at the Hotel Metropole. My friend, Gill, (4) *meets/is meeting/is going to meet* me at the airport. We (5) *eat/are eating/are going to eat* with some friends of hers in the evening. While in Toronto, I (6) *visit/am visiting/am going to visit* as many of the sights as possible, so perhaps we could meet up one afternoon if you are free. Give me a ring at the hotel.

Best wishes, Beth.

READING

Look at the information about trains from Stansted and Heathrow airports into London, and the map on page 84.

With your partner decide what Gianna and Angelo have to do to get to Dave's house.

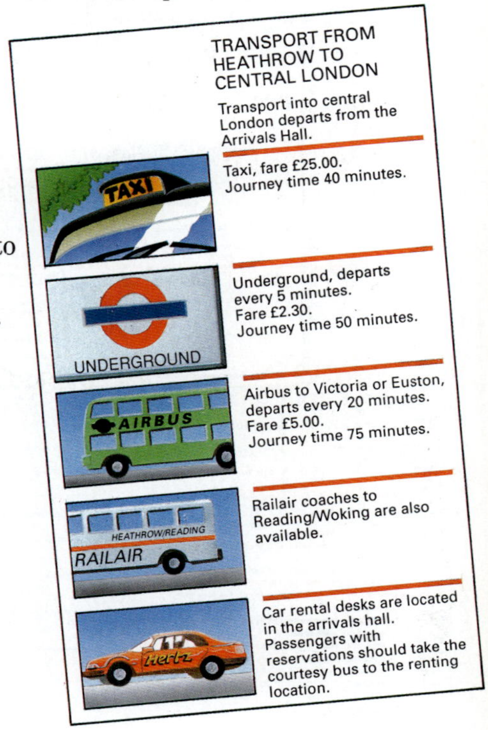
TRANSPORT FROM HEATHROW TO CENTRAL LONDON

Transport into central London departs from the Arrivals Hall.

Taxi, fare £25.00. Journey time 40 minutes.

Underground, departs every 5 minutes. Fare £2.30. Journey time 50 minutes.

Airbus to Victoria or Euston, departs every 20 minutes. Fare £5.00. Journey time 75 minutes.

Railair coaches to Reading/Woking are also available.

Car rental desks are located in the arrivals hall. Passengers with reservations should take the courtesy bus to the renting location.

From London Liverpool Street		From Stansted Airport at	
	0530§	0600§	0630§
0600§	0630†	0700†	0720§
0700	0730	0730≠	0740§
0800	0830	0800	0830
0900	0930	0900	0930
1000	1030	1000	1030
1100	1130	1100	1130
1200	1230	1200	1230
1300	1330	1300	1330
1400	1430	1400	1430
1500	1530	1500	1530
1600	1630	1600	1630
1700	1730	1700	1730
1800	1830	1800	1830
1900	1930	1900	1930
2000		2000	2030
2100		2100	
2200		2200	
2300		2300	

† Not Sunday
§ Not Saturday or Sunday
≠ Saturdays and Sundays only

All trains call at Tottenham Hale for Victoria Line ⊖ Connections
41 minutes journey time

WRITING

Now complete this fax message from Dave to Gianna. Give information about:

- the times of the trains
- the length of the journey
- where to change
- how to get from the underground to Dave's house

213 Warner Road
Walthamstow
London E17

Dear Gianna,
When you get to Stanstead Airport, you have to
....
....
....

When Angelo gets to Heathrow Airport
....
....
....

Looking forward to seeing you both soon.

Dave.

REVISION TEST 6

1 Read this article about how holidays can sometimes help people with stress and choose the best answer to the questions which follow.

Pack up your troubles and leave stress behind. A holiday could be the answer but the problems may go deeper.

by Neville Hodgkinson Medical Editor

ARE holidays really an antidote to stress? Doctors have revealed that they are prescribing holiday brochures rather than pills to cope with an increase in stress-related illness.

Even a short break can make all the difference between staying on top and going under, they say in a survey published in Doctor newspaper.

Most of us would agree that a fortnight in sun-kissed Florida is preferable to a course of tranquillisers — including the Association of British Travel Agents, who sponsored the survey.

Overwork

But are we right? Top psychologist Professor Hans Eysenck, of London's Institute of Psychiatry, says it depends very much on where the stress originates.

"If it's from overwork, a break can be helpful.

"But if the stress arises from difficulties in the way a person interacts with others, as is very often the case, I don't see that holidays would make much difference.

"If the problems are between partners, and they go away together, it will make matters even worse. Or if an individual has a lot of troubles, he may brood even more.

"The real point about stress is that many people don't know how to cope. That is the devastating nature of it. They need to learn better ways of handling themselves — but the average GP isn't really trained to help in that way.

"A holiday is no more a solution than Valium."

According to London cardiologist Dr Peter Nixon, a holiday can be "marvellously recuperative" in recovering from tiredness arising from hard work.

But when the patient's problems go deeper than that, there are dangers.

"Someone who is really over the top, who has been pumping up a lot of adrenalin in an effort of will to keep going, may go on holiday feeling restless and overactive.

"If he shoots off to the South of France and tries to live it up there, he may become even more depleted and end up seriously ill.

"Stress tends to be regarded as a kind of disease which simply needs a holiday to root it out, but it is not like that.

Retreat

"A break might help you to detach from problems for a while, but that won't remove them."

For such people, Dr Nixon says, the secret of successful recuperation is not to chase a new range of stimulating experiences but to seek out a holiday that will give them a chance to think through their problems — "something in the way of a retreat into peace and quiet.

"In medieval times it was called a state of grace, when a knight would withdraw before combat to get himself in order, ready to win or be killed the next day.

"Ancient prophets used to do the same, going into the wilderness to reconsider their position, then coming back in strength."

The nearest parallel today would probably be backpacking through the country. The quietness there would give stress sufferes that vital chance to think straight.

1 According to The Doctor newspaper, people with stress can be helped
- A only by taking holidays.
- B by taking holidays, not pills.
- C by taking a holiday in Florida.
- D by looking at holiday brochures.

2 Professor Eysenck thinks that holidays
- A are good for people who work too hard.
- B with partners should be avoided.
- C help people to interact with others.
- D do not help people to deal with stress.

3 Dr Peter Nixon thinks that holidays can be dangerous for people who
- A go to the South of France.
- B are seriously ill.
- C work too hard.
- D choose an active holiday.

4 Dr Nixon believes that people who suffer from stress should choose
- A a peaceful holiday.
- B a new type of holiday.
- C a camping holiday.
- D a holiday with friends.

2 Complete each of the following sentences with one word or expression formed from PACK.

Example: They arrived at the hotel and immediately started *unpacking* their suitcases.

1 She went on a _______ tour where everything was included in the price.
2 The airport lounge was _______ with delayed holidaymakers.
3 A _______ lunch is included in the price of the day trip.
4 Before _______ your suitcase, it's a good idea to make a list of the things you want to take.
5 Don't forget ________ your new sunglasses before you leave.

3 Complete each of the following sentences by putting one preposition in each of the spaces.

Example: He wanted to call *on* an old friend while he was visiting the city.

1 The ship calls ________ several islands in the Aegean during the cruise.
2 The bad weather meant that the picnic lunch had to be called ________ .
3 We called _______John in the car as no public transport goes to the village on Sundays.
4 In the middle of dinner the doctor was called _______ to an emergency.
5 It is a dangerous road and calls _______ extreme caution on the part of drivers.

4 You will hear a customer in a travel agency asking about holiday insurance. For questions 1 - 6 tick (✓) whether the statements are true or false.

1 Insurance is not included in the price of the holiday.
2 He is staying in Madrid for less than 17 nights.
3 The insurance includes medical expenses but not an air ambulance.
4 If you miss your flight you get £1500.
5 If your plane is delayed for up to 12 hours, you get money from the insurance company.
6 You are insured for £1000 cash if your wallet is stolen.

True	False

UNIT 7

WHAT'S COOKING

SPEAKING

1 Look at these three pictures. With your partner, decide:

Where the people are.
What they are eating.
How they feel.
Which of the meals you would prefer and why.
If some types of meal are more suitable in certain situations than others.

2 Make a list of the type of food you associate with the following:

Your country.
Great Britain.
The USA.
Another country you know about.

①

②

③

3 What is good or bad about the food of each of these countries? Are there any differences in the way people eat in these countries?

Talk about the following:

Times of meals.
Size of meals.
Eating out.
Eating at home.
The formality of meals.
Ways of preparing food.
Ways of buying and selling food.

READING

1 Look at this leaflet which advises British people about how to improve their diet. Read Part One and decide if each piece of advice would also apply to people in your country.

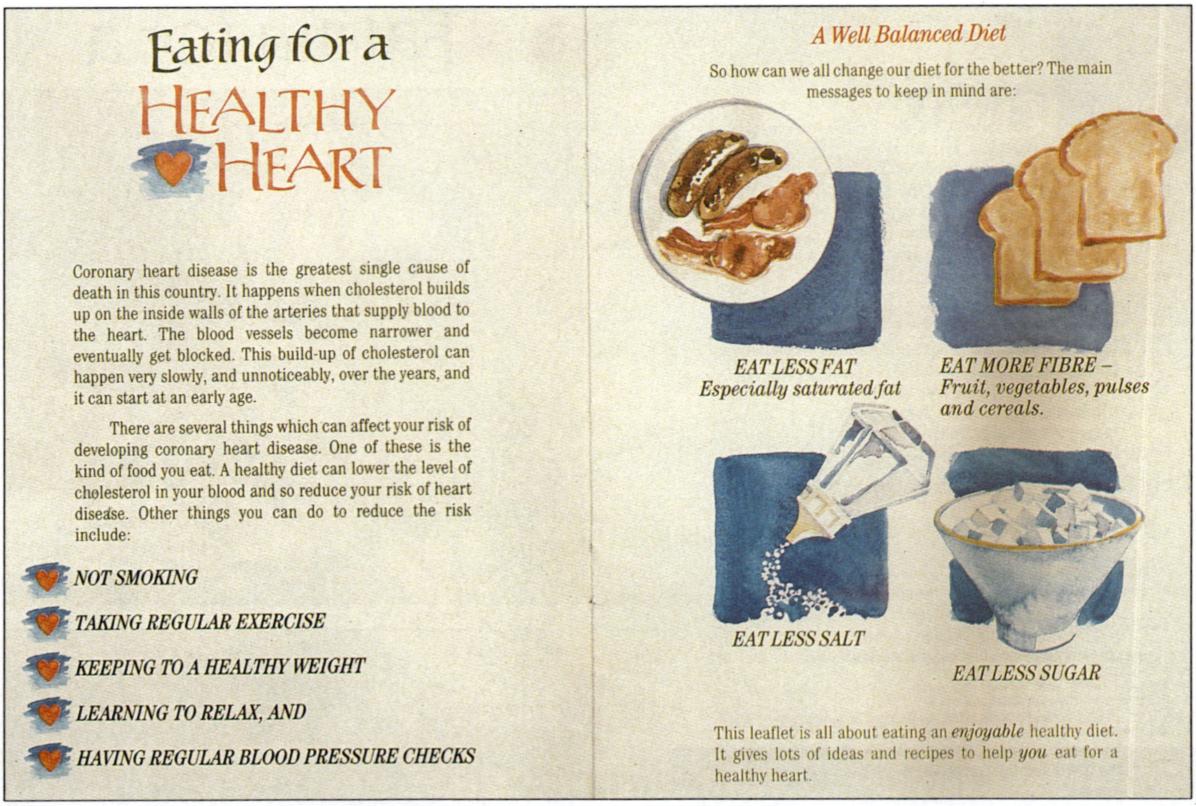

Eating for a HEALTHY HEART

Coronary heart disease is the greatest single cause of death in this country. It happens when cholesterol builds up on the inside walls of the arteries that supply blood to the heart. The blood vessels become narrower and eventually get blocked. This build-up of cholesterol can happen very slowly, and unnoticeably, over the years, and it can start at an early age.

There are several things which can affect your risk of developing coronary heart disease. One of these is the kind of food you eat. A healthy diet can lower the level of cholesterol in your blood and so reduce your risk of heart disease. Other things you can do to reduce the risk include:

- *NOT SMOKING*
- *TAKING REGULAR EXERCISE*
- *KEEPING TO A HEALTHY WEIGHT*
- *LEARNING TO RELAX, AND*
- *HAVING REGULAR BLOOD PRESSURE CHECKS*

A Well Balanced Diet

So how can we all change our diet for the better? The main messages to keep in mind are:

EAT LESS FAT
Especially saturated fat

EAT MORE FIBRE – Fruit, vegetables, pulses and cereals.

EAT LESS SALT

EAT LESS SUGAR

This leaflet is all about eating an *enjoyable* healthy diet. It gives lots of ideas and recipes to help *you* eat for a healthy heart.

Part One

2 Find words or expressions in Part One of the leaflet which mean

1 one and only
2 provide
3 not so wide
4 in the end
5 obstructed
6 accumulation
7 without anyone realising
8 influence
9 reduce

3 How do you think it's possible to reduce the amount of salt and sugar in your diet? Make a list of suggestions with your partner.

4 Decide who is student A and who is student B.

Student A should read Part Two of the leaflet, **Student B** should read Part Three of the leaflet and answer these questions:

1 Find two reasons for eating less sugar/salt.

2 What simple changes to your diet are suggested?

3 How relevant are these suggestions to your country?

5 Now tell your partner what you have found out.
Without copying from the leaflet, complete each of the paragraphs which follow in your own words. Write about either salt or sugar.

Part Two

SUGAR

Eating too much sugar can mean that you're more likely to become obese and that means a higher risk of getting heart disease. Sugar may taste good, but of course it contains nothing but calories. And, because sugary foods don't fill you up for long, it is all too easy to eat too much. In this country we tend to eat a lot of sugar, so we should cut down where possible, unless underweight.

SIMPLE CHANGES

Try to drink your tea and coffee without sugar. You might find it easier to cut down gradually.

Use unsweetened fruit juice or low calorie soft drinks rather than ordinary drinks which have a lot of sugar.

Choose fresh fruit or canned fruit in natural fruit juice rather than syrup, as an optional dessert.

Go easy on sweets, chocolates and biscuits. (In many cases this also helps cut down on fat too.)

Use less sugar in your cooking. It work for most recipes except jam and meringues.

When reading food labels, make sure sugar is not one of the ingredients at the top of the list, since ingredients are listed in order of quantity.

SALT

Everyone needs some salt but not nearly as much as many people actually eat. Too much salt has been linked with high blood pressure, which in turn can cause heart disease. So cut down on salt whenever you can.

SIMPLE CHANGES

Use less salt in cooking and measure the amount.

Try flavouring your food with lemon juice, herbs, spices or mustard, instead of salt.

Try to get out of the habit of adding salt at the table.

Cut down on salty snacks, such as salted crisps and nuts.

Try to avoid those canned and packet soups which are high in salt.

Part Three

1 It is a good idea to cut down on salt/sugar because ______________________________

____

2 One good way of doing this is to __________

____

____

3 Another good way is to ______________

____

____

GRAMMAR GR p181
Gerund and Infinitive

You *risk getting* heart disease.

We *tend to eat* a lot of sugar.

1 Notice that some verbs are followed by an infinitive (to do) and others by a gerund (doing).

In each of the following sentences choose which is best, gerund or infinitive.

Example: Try to stop (eating/to eat) so many salty snacks.

1 I enjoy (reading/to read) books about nutrition.
2 I plan (going/to go) on a diet after the holiday.
3 I need (reducing/to reduce) the amount of fats in my diet.
4 I promise (cutting down/to cut down) on sugar in tea and coffee.
5 I suggest (changing/to change) your eating habits.
6 He postponed (going/to go) to the doctor although he often felt ill.
7 He was advised (going/to go) on a high fibre diet.
8 He refused (giving up/to give up) smoking.
9 You're more likely (becoming/to become) overweight if you eat chocolates.
10 Avoid (buying/to buy) too many cakes.

LISTENING 1

You will hear an interview with Dr Cooper, a prominent dietician, talking about the British diet.

Listen and choose the best answer A, B, C or D for these questions.

1 The British have an unhealthy diet because they
- A don't know how to prepare simple foods.
- B eat their meals in front of the television.
- C don't know much about what a healthy diet is.
- D don't have much time to cook proper meals.

2 How does the food industry defend junk food?
- A They say it is high in vitamins and minerals.
- B They say nobody eats very much of it.
- C They say it's only one part of people's diet.
- D They say it's made from healthy ingredients.

3 What did the Glasgow research show?
- A People rarely eat processed foods.
- B Most people never eat fruit and vegetables.
- C Many people eat very little fresh food.
- D People don't eat at regular times.

4 Why is junk food bad for your health?
- A It isn't made from fruit and vegetables.
- B It doesn't contain important vitamins and fibre.
- C It doesn't provide enough sugar or fat.
- D It's much more expensive than simple food.

5 What does Dr Cooper advise?
- A Watch less television.
- B Give up eating junk food.
- C Avoid food which is advertised.
- D Eat a variety of different foods.

GRAMMAR GR p182

Too/Enough

1 Look at these sentences from the listening text:

*People eat **too** much junk food*
*People don't eat **enough** fibre*
*If your diet is varied **enough**, there's no problem*
*We are **too** ready to be influenced by advertising*

When do we use *too* and *enough* with nouns and adjectives?

2 Rewrite each of the following sentences in such a way that it means exactly the same as the sentence printed before it.

Example: There's too much sugar in this coffee.
This coffee is <u>too sweet</u>.

1 These vegetables are too hard; they're undercooked.
These vegetables haven't ______________

2 This salad is too oily.
There's too ______________

3 This cake is too stale for me to eat.
This cake isn't ______________

4 This hotel is too expensive for us.
This hotel costs ______________

5 There's too little cheese for four people.
There isn't ______________

6 There are too few glasses for everyone to have a drink.
We haven't got ______________

7 It's a bit too cold to eat outside this evening.
It's not ______________

8 Joanne eats too quickly.
Joanne doesn't ______________

LISTENING 2

1 Look at these verbs used to describe how food is prepared and cooked. Using your dictionary if necessary, divide the verbs in the box into those that talk about:

cutting	*mixing*	*heating*	*other*

grill	**knead**	**carve**	**roast**
mince	**fry**	**beat**	**dice**
stir	**slice**	**pour**	**bake**
boil	**chop**	**shred**	**simmer**
add	**peel**	**melt**	**grate**

①

②

③

④

⑤

⑥

⑦

2 Look at the photographs and talk about the food in each one.

What ingredients does it contain?
How do you make it?
When would you eat it?
Do you like this kind of food?

3 These are some of the instructions for making the food in one of the pictures. They are in the wrong order. With your partner decide which food is being described.

Listen and put the instructions into the correct order.

a pour the mixture into a square container
b decorate each piece with a nut
c beat the eggs into this mixture one at a time
d spread it all over the top
e take it out and leave it to cool
f melt some butter and pour it into a bowl
g put the pieces into a bowl
h cook it in the oven for forty minutes
i melt the chocolate over some warm water
j stir in the flour and cocoa and add some nuts
k cut the cake into twelve pieces
l break a bar of chocolate into pieces
m add the sugar and stir
n beat in one egg and some sugar

4 Use the verbs above to help you write the recipe for a dish from your country.

GRAMMAR GR p182

Conditionals 1

1 Look at these phrases from the listening text:

If you don't have any pecans, the other sort will be quite alright
If you boil chocolate, you spoil the taste

1 What tenses are used in these sentences?
2 What time is referred to?

Compare:

	Tense	Time
If it rains, I'll take an umbrella	1st conditional if + present subject + will	I think it will probably rain tomorrow
If/When it rains, I take an umbrella	zero conditional if + present subject + present	always (time not specific)
If I eat a lot of chocolate, I'll put on weight	1st conditional	I have the chance to eat a lot of chocolate now
If I eat a lot of chocolate, I put on weight	zero conditional	always / every time

2 In the following sentences change the main verb to either the present tense or *will* to show if it is what usually happens, or if it is related to real future time.

1 If I hear a noise in the night, I _______ (get up) to see what it is.
2 If I am on holiday, I usually _______ (eat) less.
3 If it rains tomorrow, I _______ (stay) at home.
4 If that letter doesn't arrive soon, I _______ (phone) them.
5 If pasta is cooked for too long, it _______ (become) uneatable.
6 If you cook that pasta for too long, it _______ (become) soft.
7 If you eat too much fruit, you _______ (get) stomach-ache.
8 If you eat all that fruit, you _______ (get) stomach-ache.
9 If you skip breakfast, you _______ (eat) more snacks.
10 If you leave ice cream out of the fridge, it _______ (melt).
11 If you leave that ice cream out of the fridge, it _______ (melt).
12 If you grow your own vegetables, you _______ (save) a lot of money.

3 Look back at questions 1 – 12 and decide where both zero and first conditional sentences are possible.

4 Your class has decided to organise a meal out in a restaurant next week.

1 Look at the information below, and write some sentences about each of the restaurants using the first conditional.

Examples:
If we go to La Rustica we'll be able to have a pizza.
If we go to The Taverna, we'll get a 10% discount.

Pizzeria La Rustica *eat with us or takeaway pizza, pasta and pudding, jazz nightly until 2am, young lively atmosphere no reservations - come early to get a good table reductions for groups, open all day, every day.*

The Jade Garden *authentic Cantonese and Indonesian dishes vegetarian specialities small candle-lit tables private room for groups (advance booking only).* Last orders 10.30. Indonesian music and dancing on Wednesdays. All major credit cards accepted.

The Taverna *full range of traditional Greek food a special vegetarian dish each day, tables outdoors for up to 10 people 10% discount for parties of 6 or more.* Good old-fashioned service open late on Friday and Saturday, we guarantee no loud music or entertainment - come and relax!

Yeoman of the Guard *best of British cooking beef, lamb or turkey - serve yourself at the carvery, eat as much as you like for £12 (drinks and VAT extra).* Choice of chips, roast potatoes or a green vegetable large range of hot desserts with custard, perfect for wedding aniversaries & family occasions. 19.00 – 21.30, Mon – Sat.

2 Decide who is student A, B, C and D. Discuss together which restaurant you would like to go to.

Look at the language in the box before you start.

Student A: You would like to try something different, and experience the food of another culture.

Student B: You are a vegetarian and would like a restaurant that has a choice of non-meat dishes.

Student C: You don't mind what you eat, but you would like some entertainment or live music.

Student D: You would like a quiet place with good service and a varied choice on the menu.

Preferences

I prefer eating Greek food to French food.

I'd prefer to go to a Greek restaurant.

I'd rather eat Greek food.

3 Write 3 paragraphs of 50 words each, explaining why you have made your choice. Begin each paragraph like this:

I don't think we should go to ________________
____
____
____

Nor should we go to ________________
____
____
____

I'd rather go ________________
____
____
____

5 Look at these sentences from a discussion about restaurants.

If the owner is Spanish, they'll serve traditional Spanish food.

Unless the owner is Italian, they won't serve traditional Italian food.

1 What is the difference between *if* and *unless?*

2 Put *if* or *unless* into each of these sentences about the restaurants.

a _______ we go to Yeoman of the Guard, we'll be able to eat British food.

b _______ it doesn't rain, we'll be able to sit outside at The Taverna.

c _______ we go to La Rustica early, we won't get a good table.

d _______ we serve ourselves at the carvery, we can eat as much as we like.

e _______ we go to The Jade Garden, we won't get to hear any jazz.

6 Finish each of the following sentences in such a way that it means exactly the same as the sentence printed before it.

1 We won't get a table at that restaurant unless we book in advance.

If we ______________________________

2 If he doesn't study harder, he won't pass the exam.

Unless ______________________________

3 You'll find the hotel if you follow my directions exactly.

Unless ______________________________

4 Unless one of you has got a car, you can't go to that restaurant in the country.

If ______________________________

5 Unless I have a glass of water, I'll faint.

If ______________________________

LISTENING 3

1 Look at the menu for this restaurant. With your partner check that you understand all the vocabulary.

2 Listen to the conversation and circle on the menu the food and drink which the man and woman choose.

3 Listen again and write down the questions the waiter asks when he comes to take the order.

4 Look at the menu again and in groups of three act out the situation. Student A is the waiter and Students B and C are customers ordering a meal.

5 Look at the advertisement for Simon's Restaurant.

Your class has decided to go to Simon's Restaurant for a meal and you want to get the 12% discount. With your partners decide which dishes you think should be included in the 'Mini-menu' to provide a good choice for the whole group.

Simon's RESTAURANT

Fantastic group discount with our 'Mini-menu' offer!!

For groups of 12 or more we offer a special 'Mini-menu' scheme with a discount of 12%.

All you have to do is book your table at least three days in advance and at the time of booking tell us which of our dishes you want on your special 'Mini-menu'.

You can choose 2 starters, 3 main courses and 2 desserts from our main selection for your 'Mini-menu'.

Then, when you come to eat with us, your group must select their lunch or dinner only from among those dishes.

You all get a 12% discount!

STARTERS

SOUP OF THE DAY	£1.90
EGG & PRAWN MAYONNAISE	£2.80
GARLIC BREAD	£1.80
FRIED MUSHROOMS WITH GARLIC SAUCE	£3.10
CHEF'S PRAWN COCKTAIL	£2.90
AVOCADO VINAIGRETTE	£2.95

MAIN COURSES

STEAKS served with French fries & fresh vegetables

PEPPERED FILLET STEAK	£8.70
GRILLED T-BONE STEAK	£8.20

OMELETTES served with French fries

PLAIN OMELETTE	£4.95
MUSHROOM OR HAM	£4.20

CHICKEN served with French fries or jacket potatoes

½ ROAST CHICKEN	£6.60
CHICKEN KIEV	£6.85
CHICKEN RISOTTO	£4.75
CHICKEN KEBAB	£5.65

FISH served with French fries or rice

FRIED COD	£3.95
SOLE WITH GARLIC & CREAM SAUCE	£5.75

SALADS

MIXED SALAD	£1.95
SPECIAL CALIFORNIAN SALAD	£5.10
CHEF'S UNLIMITED SALAD (EAT AS MUCH AS YOU WANT)	£5.90

DESSERTS

APPLE PIE WITH ICE CREAM	£2.10
FRESH PINEAPPLE	£2.50
CHOCOLATE PUDDING WITH HOT CHOCOLATE SAUCE	£2.70
FRIED BANANA WITH CREAM & CHOCOLATE SAUCE	£2.10
BLACK FOREST GATEAU	£2.35

TO DRINK

MALVERN SPARKLING MINERAL WATER (BOTTLE)	£1.35
HIGHLAND STILL MINERAL WATER (BOTTLE)	£1.35
ORANGE JUICE	£1.10
SPARKLING APPLE JUICE	£1.10

WINES

HOUSE WINE (RED or WHITE)

GLASS	£1.70
½ CARAFE	£4.20
CARAFE	£8.10

GRAMMAR *GR p182*

Future Time 2

1 Look at these phrases from the listening text. Which tense is used and why?

I'll have an orange juice, please　　*I'll have the Unlimited Salad*

We use *will* + *infinitive* when we make decisions, offers and promises at the time of speaking.

2 Compare these phrases:

	Time of decision
1 A: I'm going to have an ice-cream . B: What flavour?	I've already decided
A: Umm... I'm not sure, let's see the list.... . ..I know... I'll have raspberry.	I decide now
2 A: I'm doing some shopping for Mary this morning.	Already arranged
B: Oh, I'll take you in the car.	Offer now
3 A: I'm leaving tomorrow. The train goes at 9.00 in the morning.	Already arranged
B: Do keep in touch.	
A: Yes, I will. I'll write often.	I promise now

3 In each of the following sentences decide which tense is most appropriate.

> **Present Simple** - timetables and fixed times
>
> **Present Continuous** - arrangements
>
> **Going to + infinitive** - intentions
>
> **Will + infinitive** - decisions, offers, promises

1 My friend ________ (come) to visit me this weekend.

2 'I'm so busy. I never get time to clean my car.'
'I ________ (do) it for you.'

3 John ________ (come) to clean my car for me tomorrow, as I never have time.

4 I ________ (look) around the shops. Do you want anything?

5 'Would you like to order now?'
'Yes, we ________ (have) steak and chips, please.'

6 'You still haven't tidied your room although I've been asking you for ages'.
'I ________ (do) it this weekend, honestly!'

7 'When ________ (leave)?'
'Next Sunday, I ________ (get) the train to London and then ________ (fly) to Paris.'
'What time ________ (be) your train?'
'It ________ (leave) at 9am and ________ (stop) at every station. It ________ (take) two hours!'
'Oh, no! I ________ (give) you a lift to the airport in my car.'
'That's great, thank you.'

8 I can't come on Sunday. I ________ (give) Rose a lift to the airport.

9 'Don't forget to ring me and tell me what time to expect you.'
'Don't worry, I ________ (forget).'

WRITING

Speech

1 This is the speech given to a group of students who have just arrived in Britain for a three-week English course at a language school. Read the speech and answer the questions below.

1 Give each paragraph a title.
2 Look at the words which are circled. How are they important?
3 Look at the words which are underlined. How are they important?
4 A speech normally uses quite formal language. Can you find examples of informal language in the text?

Good morning. I'd like to welcome you all to Britain and wish you all a very pleasant stay. I'd also like to give you some advice this morning, which I hope will help you prepare for some of the problems you may come across.
Firstly, let me introduce myself, my name's Mary Murray and I'm the Accommodation and Welfare Officer here at the Bigtown School of Languages. So, if you have any problems about your host family, you should come straight to me.
Secondly, I'd like to inform you about mealtimes. Most British families eat at around six o'clock in the evening. Now, this may seem very early to you, but it is normal here and so please try to be back with the family in time for meals.
Then, I'd like to warn you about bathrooms! This is the area that causes most problems from the family's point of view. Please don't spend too long in the bathroom in the morning, and ask your family when would be the best time to have baths or showers
Next, I'd like to ask you to be considerate if you're coming in late at night. Your family will probably give you a key, but please try not to make a lot of noise if you come in after the family has gone to bed.
So, finally, let me thank you for listening to my speech and try to remember what I've said, because if we avoid these little problems, then everybody will have a happier stay. Thank you.

2 Choose one of the following composition titles.

1 You have been asked to make a speech welcoming a group of fifteen-year-old students who are spending one week in your town. Give them some useful advice and information. Write what you say.

2 You have been asked to begin a class discussion on the subject 'What makes a balanced diet?' Make a short speech summarising the argument. Write what you say.

3 Before you write make a plan for your composition below.

Paragraph 1: Introduction
2:
3:
4:
5: Conclusion

REVISION TEST 7

1 For each question 1–10 you must choose the word or phrase that best completes the sentence.

1 Try flavouring your food with herbs ________of salt.
A rather **B** substitute **C** instead **D** replacing

2 Her father tried to stop her ________ so many chocolates.
A eating **B** eaten **C** eats **D** ate

3 When ________ your meal, you must choose at least one main dish.
A having ordered **B** being ordered **C** ordering **D** ordered

4 They ________ the starter when he arrived.
A were serving **B** has served **C** should serve **D** serves

5 After dinner, our host ________ a speech to welcome us.
A told **B** made **C** said **D** did

6 If you tell me the name of the restaurant, I ________ you there.
A will see **B** see **C** saw **D** would see

7 We had a wonderful ________ at the hotel yesterday.
A food **B** cooking **C** service **D** meal

8 It's ________ long time since I ate Chinese food.
A very **B** so **C** such a **D** too much

9 We tend ________ much later when we are on holiday.
A eat **B** eating **C** to eating **D** to eat

10 I think it's a good idea to cut ________ on snacks between meals.
A up **B** out **C** away **D** down

2 Fill each of the numbered blanks in the following passage. Use only one word in each space.

Fifty million bottles of Lea and Perrins Worcestershire Sauce ________ (1) now sold every year in 130 different countries. The original recipe did not come ________ (2) Worcestershire, however, and at the beginning Mr Lea and Mr Perrins ________ (3) not like it.

It was Lord Marcus Sandys ________, (4) on his retirement as Governor of Bengal in India, brought the recipe ________ (5) to Worcester in 1835. He asked the local chemist's shop, Lea and Perrins, to make some up for him.

This ________ (6) did, also making some for themselves. But, deciding it tasted horrible, they put it in the cellar and ________ (7) it. Two years later, when clearing ________ (8) the cellar they found the bottles, tasted the sauce and ______(9) it was wonderful.

The sauce is ________ (10) made to the same secret recipe and the bottles you buy in the shops are about three years old. Even when 100 years old the sauce is said to be not only safe, ________ (11) also still very good indeed, despite the ________ (12) that it contains only natural ingredients.

3 Finish each of the following sentences in such a way that it means exactly the same as the sentence printed before it.

Example: I haven't laughed so much for ages.

It's ages *since I laughed so much*.

1 I get a lot of pleasure from reading cookery books.
I enjoy ______

2 The sandwiches were too stale to eat.
The sandwiches weren't ______

3 It's the first time I've eaten Yorkshire Pudding.
I've ______

4 Would you like me to cook dinner tonight?
I'll ______

5 The tea gardens are closed in wet weather.
When ______

6 How long have you been a vegetarian?
When ______

7 Don't fry food which can be grilled.
Avoid ______

8 With luck, she will win the cookery competition.
If ______

9 I'd prefer to go to a fast-food place.
I'd rather ______

10 Missing breakfast always gives me a headache.
If ______

4 Choose one of the following compositions. Your answer must be of between 120 and 180 words.

1 Describe a meal that you enjoyed very much.
2 What are the advantages and disadvantages of eating out of doors?

5 The word in capitals at the end of each of the following sentences can be used to form a word that fits suitably into the blank space. Fill each blank in this way.

1 ______ fruit juice contains no extra sugar. SWEET

2 ______ peas are often cheaper than fresh ones. FREEZE

3 ______ soups often contain a lot of salt. PACK

4 We have just bought a new gas ______. COOK

5 This food has no flavour, it's ______ . TASTE

6 This rice dish is a local ______. SPECIAL

UNIT 8 HI-TECH HORIZONS

VOCABULARY

1 Put one of these words into each of the numbered spaces in the three paragraphs below.

well	next	at	just	which
one	who	into	end	how
unable	than	tiny	in	known

PARAGRAPH 1

It is not generally (1) ________ that the first digital computer was invented (2) ________ 1835 by Charles Babbage, Professor of Mathematics (3) ________ Cambridge University. The computer programmer for this project was Ada, Countess Lovelace, (4) ________ was the daughter of the poet Lord Byron. Sadly, nineteenth-century technology was (5) ________ to fully develop Babbage's incredible discovery.

PARAGRAPH 2

I don't know (6) ________ we managed without one for so long. I (7) ________ stack all the dirty cutlery and plates (8) ________ it after meals and then switch on, usually every evening, and the things are completely clean (9) ________ day. To think for years I said I didn't want (10) ________ in the house!

PARAGRAPH 3

A Japanese company has launched a new product (11)________ it claims will probably mean the (12) ________ of public telephones. It is a (13) ________ pocket-sized phone which is no bigger (14) ________ a box of matches. It includes an automatic redial facility as (15) ________ as a ten-number memory.

2 For each paragraph, decide
a who is talking or writing.
b where you might find this text.

3 Decide which passage best describes each picture.

4 Describe one of the pictures to your partners in your own words.

1

②

③

READING

1 Look at the diagram of the Espresso coffee machine on the opposite page and put the following sentences, which describe how it works, into the correct order.

1 Making Coffee

a The only escape path for the water is through the coffee.

b When the coffee is ready to be made, a valve opens, releasing hot water into the brewing head.

c Cold water is taken from the mains water supply.

d The resulting coffee "oil" falls into the cup.

e The brewing head receives the hot water which is forced through a series of fine holes at high pressure into the coffee reservoir.

f The electric motor pumps the cold water through the boiler heat exchanger, where it is heated.

2 Making Cappuccino

a This creates steam which is trapped in the boiler under pressure.

b The electric motor pumps the cold water into the boiler.

c Cold water is taken from the mains water supply.

d The steam tap takes steam from the top of the boiler and is used to froth up milk for cappuccino coffee.

e An electric element in the boiler heats the water to about 136 degrees.

3 Read *Espresso machine* to check the order.

2 Say whether these statements are true or false.

1 The coffee has to be finely ground.
2 You have to put the exact amount of cold water into the machine.
3 You have to turn the machine off when the cup is full.
4 The filter holder holds enough coffee to make one cup.
5 Water to make coffee and steam to make cappuccino are both heated in the same boiler.

Espresso machine

ESPRESSO machines were developed and patented in Italy at the end of the last century. These machines force hot water through finely-ground coffee at a high pressure. The high pressure water forces the natural "oil" from the coffee by a process called infusion.

A portion of coffee is placed in the filter holder, which is then locked into the brewing head to make a water-tight seal. When you switch the machine on, the exact amount of cold water needed to make a single cup is pumped from the mains into the heat exchanger inside the boiler. The amount of water entering the heat exchanger is controlled by a turbine.

The hot water is then pumped to the brewing head, where it is forced through the coffee via a valve. A strong coffee liquid falls into the cup. When the correct amount of water (measured by the turbine) has been used, the control box closes the valve and stops the pump.

To froth up milk to make cappuccino coffee, the steam tap is switched on to release high-pressure steam from the boiler.

As the steam leaves the boiler, it is replaced with water from the mains. A thin metal probe in the boiler ensures that the boiler is only ever half full. The probe is charged with a small electrical current. When the water level reaches the probe, it completes an electrical circuit. This shuts down a second valve, so that no more water can enter the boiler.

A heating element inside the boiler heats the water to 136°C, producing steam. The pressure inside the boiler is controlled by a pressure gauge. When the water is cool, the pressure inside the boiler will be low, and the electrical contacts inside the pressure gauge will touch, completing an electrical circuit, so that the heating element will continue to heat the water.

3 Look at the underlined words and then use a dictionary to find the equivalent word in your own language.

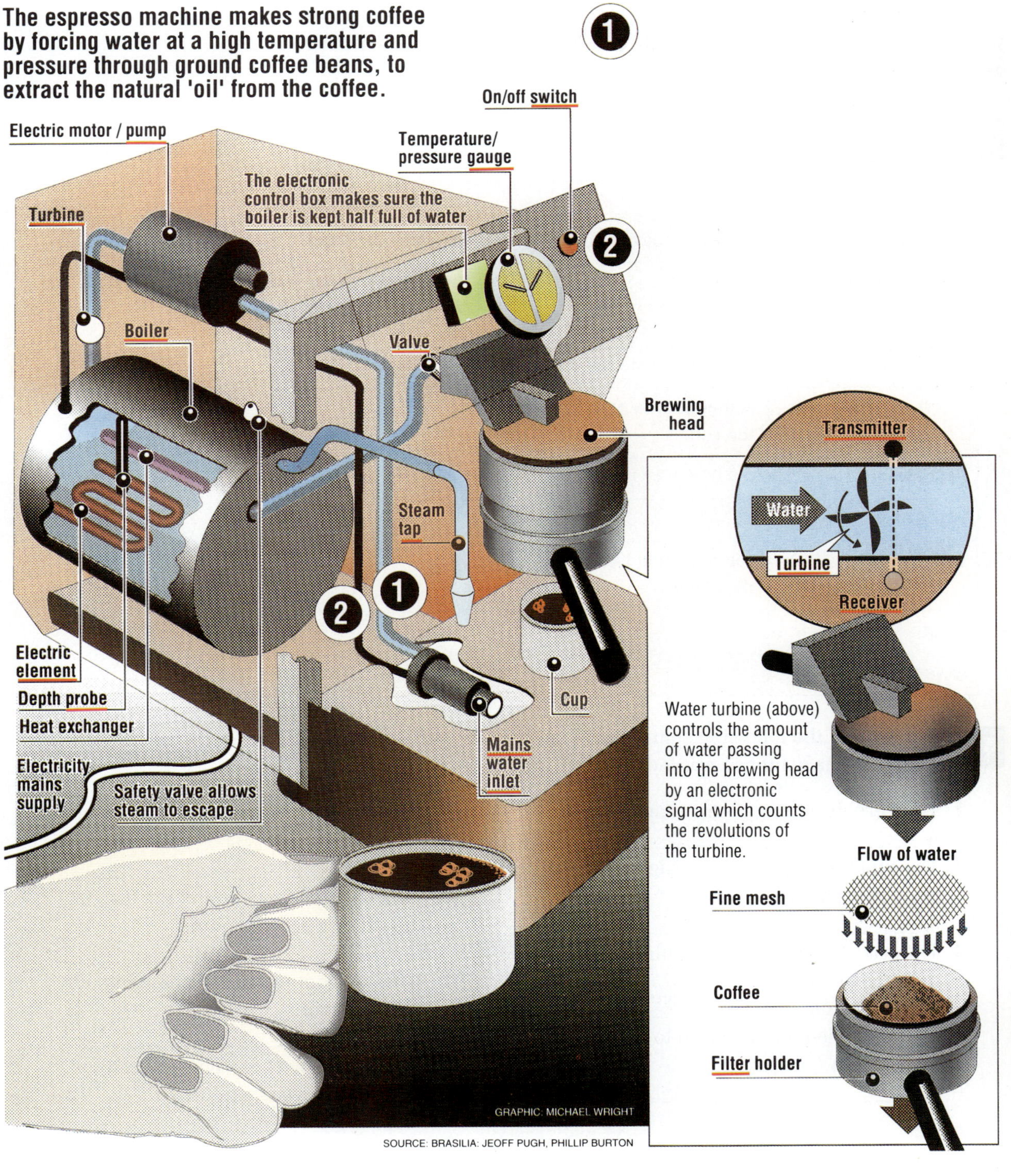

SOURCE: BRASILIA: JEOFF PUGH, PHILLIP BURTON

GRAMMAR GR p182

Passive Voice

1 Look at this sentence from the text.

Espresso machines *were developed and patented* in Italy at the end of the last century.

What verb form is used and why?

2 Read the text again more carefully and underline the verbs which are in the passive.

3 Complete this grid:
The Passive

	Active	Passive
Present Simple	someone makes the coffee	the coffee is made
Present Continuous		the coffee is being made
		the coffee has been made
Past Simple	someone made the coffee	
	someone was making the coffee	
Past Perfect		the coffee had been made
going to		
will	someone will make the coffee	
must		the coffee must be made
have to		

4 Finish each of the following sentences in such a way that it means exactly the same as the sentence printed before it.

1 They are designing a new machine.
A ______________________________

2 The building has been redesigned by a famous architect.
A ______________________________

3 They have to switch on the photocopier ten minutes before using it.
The photocopier ______________________

4 They installed a new pump to supply water to the town.
A ______________________________

5 A mechanical breakdown caused the delay.
The ______________________________

6 Someone will meet you at the airport and take you to your hotel.
You ______________________________

7 Personal computers are changing our working lives.
Our ______________________________

8 Herbs and spices have been used for cooking since early times.
People ____________________________

5 Science and Technology Quiz

Match the beginning of each sentence **1 – 16** with the end of a sentence **a – p** to make complete statements about inventions and discoveries. Try to complete the missing dates from the box.

1 The telephone	**a** was opened in Pasedena in _______
2 The first flight	**b** was devised by Sony in _______
3 The first breakfast cereal	**c** was developed by Pemberton in *1886*
4 The first McDonald's	**d** was calculated by Ptolemy in _______
5 The first traveller's cheque	**e** was invented by Bell in *1876*
6 The Walkman	**f** was transmitted by Marconi in *1895*
7 The first radio message	**g** was made by Wright in _______
8 The laws of the pendulum	**h** was first marketed in Denmark in _______
9 Coca-Cola	**i** was produced by Penguin in _______
10 Acupuncture	**j** was invented by Heinz in *1876*
11 The value of 3.1416 (π)	**k** was discovered by Columbus in _______
12 The first heart transplant	**l** were established by Galileo in _______
13 Lego	**m** has been practised in China since _______
14 The first paperback book	**n** was performed by Barnard in _______
15 The American continent	**o** was produced by Kellogg in *1893*
16 Tomato ketchup	**p** was countersigned in the USA in *1891*

2000BC
2nd Century AD
~~1886~~
1492
~~1891~~
1591
~~1876~~
1903
1935
1948
~~1893~~
~~1876~~
1955
~~1895~~
1967
1978

LISTENING 1

1 Listen to Part 1 of this conversation with the manager of Britain's largest pizza factory and put one word in each space in this passage.

The factory makes (1) ____ pizzas per week. Most are immediately (2) _____ but some are (3) ______ and then sold fresh. The most popular type is the (4) _____ - sized pizza, which accounts for about (5) _____ % of the pizzas bought in shops. This is because they are seen as (6) _____ and (7) ______.

2 Listen to part 2 of the conversation and put one of the verbs from the box in each of the spaces A – G to show the process of pizza-making in the factory.

cooked frozen stamped coated delivered assembled mixed

A [ ] → B [ ] → C [ ] → D [ ] → E [ ] → F [ ] → G [ ]

3 Which of the stages mentioned is shown in each of the four pictures opposite?

4 Listen again to check your answers and then write a sentence using the passive form of each of the verbs in the box to describe how pizzas are made in the factory.

5 Write a description of how pizzas are made in a factory. Try to use the words in the box below, and passive verb forms wherever possible.

first when then before after once finally

①

②

③

④

GRAMMAR GR p182
Agents

1 Discuss with your partner:

1 In what situations do we use the passive in English?

2 When is it necessary to use an agent (e.g. *by* someone)? Look at these examples:

a Espresso machines were developed and patented in Italy at the end of the last century.

b Cold water is taken from the mains water supply.

c America was discovered *by Columbus* in 1492.

d My friend was bitten *by a dog*.

e My car has been stolen.

3 How easy is it to change these sentences into the active form?
Why are some easier to change than others?

2 Match each of the examples above to one of these three situations in which the passive is used:

1 When the action is more important than the agent.

2 When we do not know (or do not want to say) who the agent is.

3 When we are describing a process.

3 Look at each of these active sentences. Change them to the passive, and decide whether to include the agent or not.

1 The postman has delivered a lot of letters this morning.
A ______________________________

2 Someone has stolen some money from my bag.
Some ______________________________

3 People are drinking more coffee than tea these days.
More ______________________________

4 Pizzaro first brought potatoes to Europe in 1554.
Potatoes ______________________________

5 You have to return all videos to the shop before 6 p.m.
All videos ______________________________

6 You are not permitted to smoke in the cinema.
Smoking ______________________________

7 An electric element in the boiler heats the water.
The water ______________________________

8 The company employs forty-five technicians.
Forty-five technicians ______________________________

9 Someone invented the Espresso machine in Italy.
The Espresso machine______________________________

10 Some people have not returned books to the library.
Some books ______________________________

4 Compare with your partner. In each case decide which sounds better - the active, the passive, or does it make no difference?.

READING

1 With your partner make a list of:

1 Ten objects which you think will soon be out of date (e.g. LP records, which are being replaced by CDs).

2 Ten objects you think will be important in the future.

Compare with other students.

2 Which of these things will change a lot in the next ten years, and how?

shopping and money
working and leisure
family life

3 Read the article on the next page quickly, and answer the questions below.

1 Which of the things you talked about are mentioned in the article?

2 The article is about Britain. Which of the predictions are also true for your country?

TRENDS

How will society change in the next century? Debbie Kent looks at some future trends

Forecasting the future is a risky business. But that doesn't mean we can't say anything about the next decade. In fact one trend is almost completely predictable: population growth. The population of the UK, currently just over 57 million, **is expected to** keep rising to hit 59 million by 2001. Most significant is how the structure of that 59 million will change. The number of 16 to 19-year-olds has been falling since the baby boom generation reached adolescence in the early 1980s, and it will stay low through the 90s and into the next century. On the other hand, the proportion of older people **will grow**. By 2001 more than 45% of us **will be over 50**.

Some implications are clear. Fewer school leavers and a workforce that is growing only slowly will have an impact on the labour market. Employers **may have to look** elsewhere to fill vacancies — to women with children and older people.

At the other end of the scale, the growth in the number of elderly people means a fresh look at the idea of retirement. For the first time **most of us can expect to have** 30 years of retirement to look forward to.

Although society will still be made up largely of conventional families, **there is a growing trend** for fewer stereotypical households: more homes will consists of single adults. Then there will be households split by divorce, mixed households of second marriages, and three generations living under one roof. The average household size **is predicted to fall from** 2.7 people (1981) to 2.4 people by 2001.

Finance is one of the areas that **is likely to** undergo fundamental change between now and the year 2001. If full European monetary union takes place, we **could routinely be using** a 'hard ECU' or some other denomination of Euro-wide currency even for our spending at home.

Will we be using hard currency at all? The answer is almost certainly yes, for low-value transactions and for that small but intractable section of the population that does not have a bank account. But the cheque **should be** pretty much on the way out by 2001. According to Roger Taylor of Midland Payment Transmission Services, developers of payment card systems: "Transactions will be primarily plastic-based but people won't carry as many cards."

So the walletful of plastic is likely to be replaced by a single multi-function card that will act as cheque book, credit card, cash dispenser and debit card. Haven't we got that (or almost) already? The difference is that the 2001 version will be a 'smart card' with a built-in memory. It will carry as much information about you as a personal organiser — details of bank accounts, credit ratings, insurance, salary — and will be able to pass that information on to anyone you choose to do business with.

4 Now read more carefully and decide whether the following statements are true or false.

1 There will be an increase in population.
2 The proportion of young people is going to increase.
3 The number of working women is likely to increase.
4 There will be fewer jobs for older people.
5 There will be more people living in each house.
6 Coins and banknotes will no longer exist.
7 Everybody will have a bank account.
8 Most people will use cheques to do their shopping.
9 There will be more types of credit cards in use.
10 The smart card is like a small computer.

5 Look at the phrases in the article which are in bold type and decide which of them expresses

1 something that will definitely happen
2 something which is probably going to happen
3 something that is possibly going to happen.

6 Now make predictions about the next decade using these phrases.

Talk to your partner about some of the following:

sport	the family
holidays	money
your life	the economy
social problems	food
international relations	music

7 **Composition**
In what ways do you think life will change in your country in the next ten years? How much will this affect you personally?

LISTENING 2

1 Before you listen, discuss with your partner the meanings of these words, and what you think the listening will be about.

screen credit card keyboard microchip telephone card satellite

2 You will hear a radio interview about smart cards. Listen and make a list of the advantages and disadvantages.

GRAMMAR *GR p183*

Will/Going to

1 Look at these phrases from the listening text.

*I think everyone **will have** them ten years from now.*
*From tests that have been carried out in France, we can see that **they're going to be** very popular.*
*I think people **will use** them here too.*
*It's not **going to be** long before........*

When do we use *will* and when do we use *going to* for predictions?

	When?	Why?
From the bookings we've received we can see the show is going to be popular.	future	we can see from the bookings
I'm sure the show will be a great success.	future	this is my opinion
Look at the clouds. It's going to rain.	future	we can see from the clouds
I think it will be fine this weekend	future	it's only my opinion

2 Complete these sentences using *will* or *going to*.

1 Do you think smart cards _______ become popular?

2 Hurry up, the train is already in the station. We _______ miss it.

3 Look, Clive's gone a strange colour. Do you think he _______ be sick?

4 I think Greece _______ win the next World Cup.

5 Looking at our statistics, we can predict that crime rates _______ increase in the next few years.

6 I believe there _______ be a complete change in attitudes towards money in the next decade.

7 The fortune teller who reads my palm tells me I _______ have four children.

8 Do you think Anna _______ accept the new job she has been offered?

LISTENING 3

1 Ruth and Michael are discussing the best way to reorganise their office. Listen to Part 1 and mark on the diagram the new position of the pieces of equipment below. Write the letters A - E on the diagram.

2 Listen to Part 2. Michael is talking to his boss about buying new office equipment. Write down the advantages of buying the new fax and laser printer which they mention.

Advantages of new fax :

Advantages of laser printer:

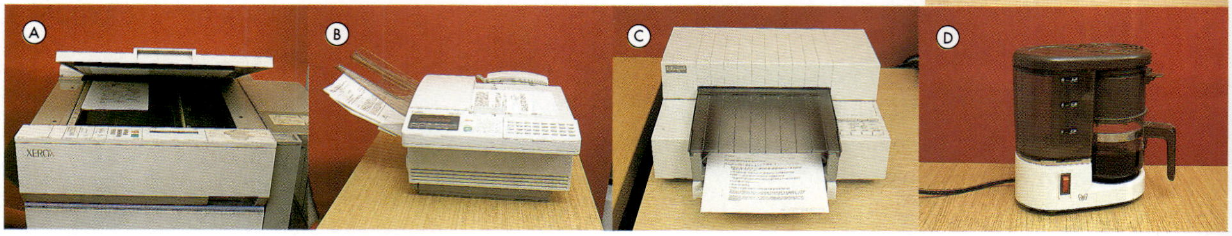

SPEAKING

Opinions

1 Look at these phrases from the listening used to give opinions and agree/disagree. Decide which of the phrases in group 2 would be an appropriate response to each phrase in group 1, and which wouldn't, and why.

1 Ways of giving an opinion:
I think we should...
I don't think we should...
In my opinion we should...
Wouldn't it be a good idea to ....?
If you ask me...

2 Ways of agreeing and disagreeing:
That's right.
So do I.
Nor do I.
Absolutely.
I think so too.
That's a good idea.
You've got a point there.
No, I'm sorry. I can't agree with you there.
I'm afraid I don't agree.

2 With your partner use the expressions above to give your opinion about some of these topics. Find out whether your partner agrees or disagrees and why.

fast food
keeping pets in a flat
ballet dancing
Picasso
preventing heart disease
nuclear power
computer games
working in an office
mass tourism
Heavy Metal

VOCABULARY

1 There are many ways of making nouns from verbs. Here are some examples:

	verb	**noun**	
a	express	expression	(verb + *sion*)
b	equip	equipment	(verb + *ment*)
c	predict	prediction	(verb + *tion*)
d	discover	discovery	(verb + *y*)

Sometimes one or two letters from the verb are changed or lost in the change.

Example: includ*e* inclu*sion*

2 Look at the verbs in the box and decide if they are the same as type **a, b, c** or **d** above. Two of the verbs are of a different type. Which type is it?

observe	explore	improve
organise	complete	assemble
connect	design	explain
solve	inform	deliver
programme	invent	distribute
encourage	develop	describe
employ	produce	calculate
replace	decide	create
destroy	discuss	

Example:

verb	type	noun
observe	**c**	observation

READING

1 Discuss with your partner what you know about global warming and the greenhouse effect.

2 Read the article quickly to find the answers to these questions:

1 What do these pairs of numbers refer to?
80 / ½ 2090 / 30 1988 / 24 150 / 24

2 What have been the main causes of global warming?

3 Read more carefully and match the underlined words from the text on the left with the meanings on the right.

Example:

heatwave ———	long period of hot weather
1 pressing	getting faster
2 build up	not really
3 hardly	covered with water
4 maintain	serious
5 accelerating	never seen before
6 dramatic	absence of water
7 flooded	disturbed
8 drought	strongly believe
9 upset	important
10 unprecedented	increase

4 Divide the following into

a *causes* of global warming
b *results* of global warming
c *solutions* to the problem of global warming

1 cutting down fewer trees
2 melting ice-caps
3 using aerosols
4 droughts in hot countries
5 eating frozen and chilled food
6 rising temperatures
7 building sea defences
8 planting more trees
9 using alternative sources of energy
10 flooding in Britain

5 Now complete the three paragraphs below in your own words. Try to use the passive form of verbs where it seems appropriate.

1 Global warming is caused by

____

____

2 This has resulted in

____

____

3 Some solutions would be

____

____

HOW THE GREENHOUSE EFFECT *WORKS*

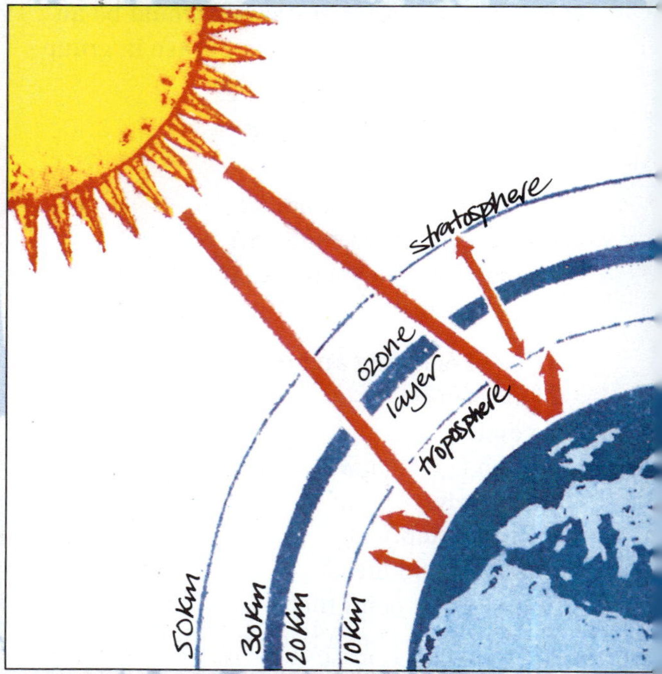

The sun's shortwave radiation can penetrate even large amounts of CO_2 and CFCs in the troposphere – the part of the atmosphere nearest the earth. These rays are reflected from the earth as longwave 'heat' radiation, much of which is trapped by the carbon dioxide and CFCs. So the climate gets warmer.

CLIMATE OF CHANGE

Of all these issues, many experts agree that the most pressing problem facing all of us, not just in Britain, is that of the gradual warming of the earth's atmosphere caused mainly by the build up of carbon dioxide and CFCs producing what has become known as the greenhouse effect. Informed opinion is that the atmosphere is getting warmer. In the past 80 years the average temperature has increased by half of one degree Celsius.

Hardly the making of a heatwave, but the consequences are likely to be significant. Weather experts maintain that the rate of increase in the warming process is accelerating. Some predict that, by 2090, the temperature in southern Britain on a typical summer's day could be 26 – 30°C (In 1988 the highest temperature recorded was 24°C.) Good news, you may think, but there'd be a price to pay.

MELTING ICE CAPS

Even a small rise in temperature could, scientists say, have a dramatic effect on ice in the polar regions. Pieces would break off, float away and melt. Sea levels would rise and Britain's low-lying coastal regions would be flooded unless sea defences were built. But the effect of higher temperatures on other countries could be even more severe.

Hot countries which are already suffering from droughts could get even hotter and drier, and more arid.

CREATING A GLOBAL GREENHOUSE

What Man has done to produce this warmer climate is to burn fossil fuels (coal, gas and oil), cut down trees faster than they are replaced, use aerosol sprays and buy food packaged in rigid-foam containers.

He's also used refrigerators and freezers with CFC coolants. Burning fossil fuels uses oxygen and produces carbon dioxide. Trees that are growing use carbon dioxide and produce oxygen. So there could be a healthy balance.

But since the industrial revolution – about 150 years ago – that balance has been upset as more fossil fuels have been burned and forests cut down and burned at an unprecedented rate. Both processes produce carbon dioxide (CO_2). The result is that carbon dioxide in the atmosphere has increased by 24% over the past 150 years. Some CO_2 is essential to life – to help plants grow and to retain some heat. But the very large amounts now present are, in part, responsible for trapping even more heat in the earth's atmosphere – the so-called 'greenhouse effect' (see illustration).

Other important 'greenhouse gases' are CFCs (chlorofluorocarbons) especially the types which have been used in aerosols, some food trays, domestic freezers and refrigerators, supermarket refrigeration systems and most air conditioning systems. Some CFCs are at least 10,000 times more powerful than carbon dioxide in trapping heat in the earth's atmosphere.

GRAMMAR *GR p183*

Conditional 2

1 Look at these pairs of sentences about global warming. For each pair say what the difference is in meaning and in form.

1 a If temperatures rise any more, the polar ice-caps will melt.
b If temperatures rose any more, the polar ice-caps would melt.

2 a If the ice-caps melt, parts of Britain will be flooded.
b If the ice-caps melted, parts of Britain would be flooded.

3 a If more trees are cut down, the level of carbon dioxide will rise.
b If more trees were cut down, the level of carbon dioxide would rise.

When do we use the first conditional and when do we use the second conditional?

2 Often we decide to use the first or the second conditional depending on how we feel about the situation. In each of these situations decide which is better for you - first or second conditional - and complete the sentences.

1 If I win / won lots of money, I will / would..

2 If it snows / snowed this winter, I will / would...

3 If I don't / didn't do my homework, I...

4 If I don't / didn't have to come to school next week, I...

5 If I can / could be a famous person for a day, I...

6 If I have / had the chance to travel next year, I...

7 If I have / had to choose a new sport or pastime to learn, I...

8 If I pass / passed the exam, I...

3 In one of the sentences only the second conditional is possible. Which one is it and why?

WRITING

Opinions

1 Read this composition on the subject of global warming, and then fill in the spaces in the plan.

Do you agree that global warming represents a serious problem for the future of the world?

1 Introduction
2 a *Scientists do not agree*
  b ________
  c ________
3 a ________
  b ________
  c ________
4 Conclusion
  Limits of our knowledge

In recent years a lot of publicity has been given to the problem of global warming caused by the so-called greenhouse effect.

It is worth pointing out, however, that not all scientists agree about the causes of warming or, indeed, if it is happening at all. Moreover, it is important to remember that reliable records have only existed for 130 years, which is a very short period in climatic terms. While the 1980s was a particularly warm decade, we know that there have been other warm, and cold, periods in history, although we have no precise records about them.

In other words, recent changes in the climate could be explained by natural variations. Besides the lack of convincing evidence, there is a tendency for this type of issue to get too much publicity and to become fashionable, which, in my opinion, does not help the scientists. Science is about making calculations and predictions and building up theories that must be tested, and often only time will tell us the real answer.

So, bearing this in mind, it is important to be aware of the possible consequences of problems like global warming, but it is also necessary to remain realistic about the nature of scientific research and the limits of our knowledge.

2 Look carefully at the underlined words. How are they important?

3 Choose one of these composition titles:

1 "Most people will soon be working from home, using a computer terminal." Do you think this is a realistic prediction?
2 Describe some of the effects of the growth of satellite TV. What are the prospects for the future?
3 Do you think it is a good idea to have a telephone in your car? Explain your reasons.

4 Find a partner who has chosen the same question as you. Find out if you agree or not.

Make a plan for your composition in the grid below.

1 Introduction
2 a ____________________
  b ____________________
  c ____________________
3 a ____________________
  b ____________________
  c ____________________
4 Conclusion

5 Before you write your composition, look again at the words underlined in the text and other similar expressions on pages 15, 70 and 71. Remember to use them in your composition.

REVISION TEST 8

1 Choose one of the following compositions. Your answer must be of between 120 and 180 words.

1 "Computerisation is changing the world for the worse not for the better." What is your opinion?
2 "Television is producing a generation which does not read, write or talk enough." Do you agree?
3 Why have most important inventions and discoveries been made by men? Do you think this will continue in the future?

2 Complete each of the following sentences with a preposition to form an expression with TURN.

Example: He turned <u>*on*</u> the machine but nothing happened.

1 The music is too loud, please turn it _______ a little.

2 Please turn _______ all lights before leaving the building.

3 Her friend turned _______ unexpectedly from abroad.

4 She hopes to turn her research _______ a popular book.

5 When I eventually met him, he turned _______ to be interested in the same field as me.

6 The weather was so bad we were forced to turn _______ and go home.

7 His application to join the tennis club was turned _______ because he was too young.

3 The word in capitals at the end of each of the following sentences can be used to form a word that fits suitably in the blank space. Fill each blank in this way.

Example: Although it rains little, the local tap water is quite <u>*drinkable*</u>. DRINK

1 The road is being _______ to cope with the increased volume of traffic. WIDE

2 The _______ of the finance department is to go ahead. COMPUTER

3 _______ of the club is open to all who live in the village. MEMBER

4 The _______ of the book led the publishers to print a second edition. POPULAR

5 Toppings on large pizzas are assembled _______ . ART

6 The factory has four _______ lines working at any one time. PRODUCE

4 Make all the changes and additions necessary to produce, from the following sets of words and phrases, sentences which together make up a complete letter. Write each sentence in the space provided.

Example: I be very surprised/receive/letter/you this morning.

I was very surprised to receive a letter from you this morning.

Dear Ms Salt

1 I/very interested/read/your article/global warming/the newspaper.

____

2 I/afraid/I not agree/you/a number of points.

____

3 Firstly,/you say/some scientists/not believe/the theory.

____

4 Who/be/these scientists? I/never/hear/them.

____

5 Secondly,/it/not true/global warming/receive/too much publicity.

____

6 On the contrary, we/need/make/public/aware/such dangers.

____

7 We/must/all put pressure/the authorities/if/ we want/something/ be done.

____

8 Lastly,/you seem/suggest/do/nothing/in case/the scientists/wrong.

____

9 Well,/if/they/right/it/be/too late/by the time/we find out.

____

Yours sincerely

Dr Pepper

UNIT 9 MIND AND BODY

VOCABULARY

1 Name all the electrical appliances you can find in the photos above.

2 How essential is each of these?
Which ones could you do without?
Which ones can't you do without?

3 In what ways can electricity be dangerous in the home?

Complete these sentences:
If you ______________________________.
If you ______________________________.
If you ______________________________.

4 Label each of these things in the pictures on the next page. PLUG, SOCKET, FLEX, ADAPTOR, SWITCH, HEATER.

5 Which of these situations do you think is the most dangerous? Why?

LISTENING 1

1 Listen to a telephone conversation and tick (✓) the pictures mentioned.

2 Listen again and answer these questions.

1 Mrs Platt is Mrs Grey's
- A friend.
- B neighbour.
- C social worker.
- D relative.

2 Mr Fields is Mrs Grey's
- A doctor.
- B friend.
- C son.
- D nephew.

3 How does Mr Fields feel about the phone call?
- A Grateful.
- B Offended.
- C Embarrassed.
- D Bored.

4 What is wrong with the sockets in Mrs Grey's house?
- A They are too loose.
- B They are not big enough.
- C There are too few of them.
- D They do not work properly.

5 What is Mr Fields going to do?
- A Take Mrs Platt's advice.
- B Ask for his aunt's opinion.
- C Visit Mrs Platt.
- D Have some work done.

GRAMMAR GR p183

So/Such

1 Look at these phrases from the listening text.

*That old house is **so** dangerous*
*These things cost **such** a lot of money*

When do we use *so* and when do we use *such*?

2 Put *so* or *such* in each of the following sentences.

1 This chocolate is ________ hard that I can't eat it.
2 It was ________ a cold night that we turned on the central heating.
3 There were ________ many people that we had to bring more chairs from upstairs.
4 It was ________ a boring talk that everyone was looking at their watches all the time.
5 It was ________ foggy weather that the airport was closed.
6 He drives ________ badly that I refuse to accept lifts from him.
7 There is ________ much smog in the air that traffic is often restricted.
8 It was ________ horrible food that nobody ate it.
9 His handwriting is ________ illegible that he has to type all his compositions.
10 It was ________ a well-organised trip that we had nothing to worry about.

play it SAFE

This Morning's Liz Earle on protecting your child in the sun

It is estimated that about half our total lifetime's sun exposure happens during childhood. Long summer holidays and lots of outdoor activities mean that children are at far greater risk of over-exposure than adults. Children's skin is very sensitive to sunburn. Not only is this painful and damaging to the skin, but just one case of severe sunburn during childhood is thought to double the risk of developing skin cancer in later life. Follow this safe tan code:

- Don't let children play outside in the midday sun without some form of protection. It may be easier to slip on a lightweight shirt and hat than to apply sunscreen.
- Look for sunscreens that have the highest SPF numbers. Don't use less than SPF 15 on young, vulnerable skins.
- Sunscreens for toddlers should say on the label that they have been especially formulated for children. These products contain fewer chemical ingredients and so are less likely to irritate children's delicate skin.
- The sun's rays pass through water, so always use the waterproof sunscreens while swimming and make sure children re-apply them frequently.
- Babies under six months should never be exposed to strong sunshine. This is because their skin hasn't fully formed the melanin-producing cells that protect the skin. Protect older babies with sun hats and pram parasols.

READING

1 Have you ever been sunburnt?
How does it feel?
How can it be prevented?

2 Read the article and decide if these sentences are true or false.

1. Children spend more time in the sun than adults.
2. Children are more likely to get skin cancer than adults.
3. Light clothes do not provide protection from strong sun.
4. Sunscreens with SPF 15 or less are best for young children.
5. You can buy special sunscreen for very young children.
6. Sunscreens contain chemicals that may irritate the skin.
7. Children should put on more sunscreen after swimming.
8. Babies get sunburned more easily than older children.

GRAMMAR GR p183
Present Perfect Continuous

1 Look at the woman in the photo.

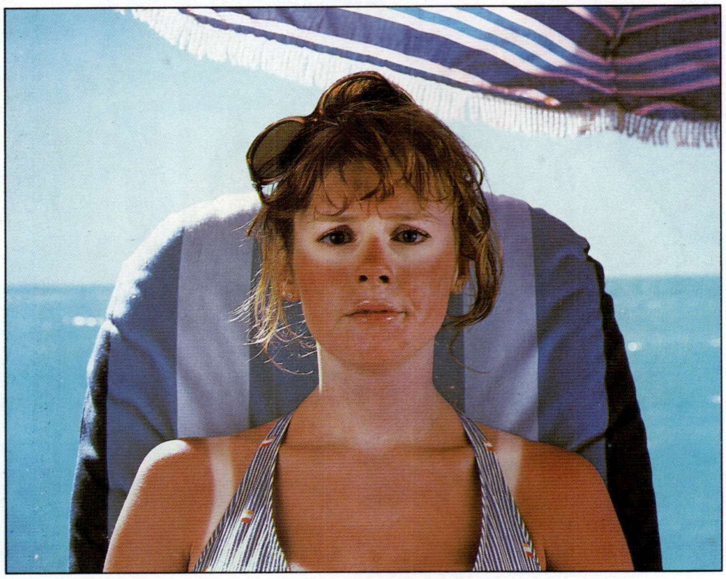

Where do you think she comes from?
Where is she now?
What mistakes has she made?
How does she feel?
Is she going to enjoy the rest of her holiday?

2 What has she been doing this morning? Make sentences like the example.

Example: She/sit/in the sun
She's been sitting in the sun

1 She/swim/a number of times.
2 She/wear/a bikini.
3 She/read/a book.
4 She/listen/music/walkman.
5 She/drink/Coke.
6 She/not sit/under an umbrella.
7 She/not use/sunscreen lotion.
8 She/sleep/in the sun.

3 Present Perfect or Present Perfect Continuous?

1 Why are the sentences in the above exercise in the Continuous form?
2 Why are the following sentences not Continuous?
   a She has just woken up.
   b She has lost her sunglasses.
   c She has finished her Coke.
   d She's already finished one book.
   e She's written four postcards.
   f She hasn't posted them yet.

4 In the following sentences decide which is best – the Present Perfect Continuous or the Present Perfect Simple, or if it makes no difference.

1 I (write) five letters this morning.
2 I (write) letters all morning.
3 I (lose) my pen somewhere in this room.
4 I (use) this sunscreen for years. It's the best.
5 Janice (work) in another office this week.
6 Janice (work) in five different offices since joining the company.
7 I (learn) English for two years.
8 Louise (phone) me twice this morning.

5 Make a note of

1 some things you have been doing this morning/ afternoon/ evening - this week or recently.

2 some things you've done in the same period.

Now tell your partner.
Do you agree with your partner's use of the Simple or Continuous form?

6 Make all the changes and additions necessary to produce, from the following sets of words and phrases, sentences which together make the complete postcard which Jenny sent to her friend Sue.

VOCABULARY

1 Complete each space with one word from the box combined with the word *sun* to form a new word.

rise	screen	roof
shine	bathing	glasses
set	tan	flower

Example: He liked to get up very early and walk along the beach at *sunrise*.

1 In the evening the clouds disappeared and there was a beautiful ________ over the sea.
2 You could tell he'd been on holiday from his deep golden ________.
3 It's difficult to read on the beach without ________.
4 It was such a nice morning he decided to have breakfast outside in the warm ________.
5 To get more air in the car she opened the ________.
6 The roof of the hotel was an excellent place to go ________.
7 The seed of the ________ is used to make cooking oil.
8 ________ is a lotion that protects your skin from burning.

LISTENING 2

Listen to the conversation and decide if each of these sentences is true or false.

1 Jenny is sorry that Sue didn't go with her.
2 Jenny bought some sunscreen before she left.
3 Jenny forgot to buy sunscreen when she arrived.
4 Jenny stayed on the beach for longer than she had intended.
5 Jenny was unable to go back to the beach but found lots of other things to do.
6 Jenny read books all day in the hotel.
7 Jenny doesn't even have a suntan.

GRAMMAR GR p183

Regrets

1 Look at these phrases from the listening text.

I wish you had come with me
I wish I'd taken a few books with me
I wish I'd stayed at home
If only I hadn't been so stupid

1 Which tense is used after *I wish* or *If only*?
2 What time is referred to?
3 What feelings are expressed?

2 Finish each of the following sentences in such a way that it means exactly the same as the sentence printed before it.

1 I regret going to bed so late last night.
I wish ________________________
2 If only I'd worked harder for my exams.
I wish ________________________
3 If only I had taken that job in the bank.
I regret ________________________
4 Jenny regrets not buying some sunscreen before her holiday.
Jenny wishes ________________________
5 He regrets not telling anyone it was his birthday.
He wishes ________________________
6 I regret not booking the seats in advance.
If only ________________________
7 I wish I'd gone on holiday with my friends.
I regret ________________________
8 They regret ever getting married.
They wish ________________________

3
1 When is it better to use *I wish* or *If only* and when is it better to use *I regret*?
2 Do you have any regrets in your life? Make a list of some of the things you regret – you can invent them if you like!

Now tell your partner.

LISTENING 3

1 What has happened to the pensioner?
2 What has happened to his money?
3 Why do you think this has happened?

Listen to this radio programme where the story is discussed, and fill in the information in the numbered spaces below.

Pensioner Leaves Secret Fortune to Aromatherapist

Mr Edward Grey, (87), of Newton Street, who died last month, has left a fortune of £1.008.279 to his local aromatherapist. Members of his family were shocked at the size of the fortune and enraged not to receive any of it.

Name	Relationship (to Mr Grey)	Amount left (in will)	Purpose	Reason
Rosemary Lacey	Aromatherapist	£1,008,279	1.	he got relief from aromatherapy
2.	nephew	£50	3.	4. ....
5.	6.	£100	to spend on second -hand furniture	7. ....
Cecilia Grey	daughter	8.	for her old age	9. ....

GRAMMAR GR p184

Conditional 3

1 Look at these sentences from the listening text and answer the questions.

1 If he'd paid back the £50, he would have inherited a much larger sum.
A Did he inherit a larger sum?
B Why was this?
C Can he change the situation?

2 If she'd been more patient, she'd have got the furniture.
A Did she get the furniture?
B Why was this?
C Can she change the situation?

3 If she'd agreed to look after him, she'd have inherited the house.
A Did she inherit the house?
B Why was this?
C Can she change the situation?

4 Which tenses are used in third conditional sentences?
What time do they refer to?

2 Read this article.
Why did June Booker have to go to hospital twice in one day?

WHAT A BARGAIN

When June Booker bought a new frying pan at 30% off in the sales, she thought she had got a real bargain. But as it turned out that was only the beginning of a very expensive day. First, she dropped the pan on her foot on the way home and was taken to hospital. 'I had lots of shopping because I hadn't planned to buy a frying pan, and the pan was very heavy, I just couldn't carry it all.' said June. At the hospital her foot was bandaged and she was sent home in a taxi.

Then, when she eventually got home, she decided to use the new pan to cook dinner. 'I'd just put some oil in it and started to heat it up when the phone rang. I only left the kitchen for a couple of minutes but when when I came back there were flames coming out of it' said June. So she picked up a bowl of water and threw it onto the pan. 'I know it was a stupid thing to do, but I panicked,' said June, 'and the flames got bigger.'

Fortunately, her neighbours saw smoke and called the fire brigade, who arrived and dealt with the fire in minutes. Although she will need a new kitchen, the rest of June Booker's flat was only slightly damaged by smoke. A shocked but unhurt Mrs Booker was taken to hospital for routine tests. 'They were rather surprised to see me back again so soon.' she said.

3 Complete each of the phrases from **A** with one of the phrases from **B** to make a third conditional sentence about the story. The first one has been done for you as an example.

A

1. If Mrs Booker hadn't bought a frying pan in the sale, [e]
2. If the frying pan hadn't been in the sale, [ ]
3. If she hadn't dropped the pan on her foot, [ ]
4. If the pan hadn't been heavy, [ ]
5. If she had had less shopping, [ ]
6. If the phone hadn't rung, [ ]
7. If she hadn't panicked, [ ]
8. If she hadn't thrown water onto the pan, [ ]
9. If her neighbours hadn't seen smoke, [ ]
10. If the fire brigade hadn't come so quickly, [ ]
11. If she had turned off the cooker, [ ]

B

a they wouldn't have called the fire brigade.
b she wouldn't have dropped the pan.
c she wouldn't have left the kitchen.
d it wouldn't have hurt her foot.
e she wouldn't have gone to hospital twice in one day.
f the rest of the flat could have been seriously damaged.
g the oil wouldn't have caught fire.
h she wouldn't have been taken to hospital.
i Mrs Booker wouldn't have bought it.
j she wouldn't have thrown water into the pan.
k the flames wouldn't have spread.

4 Finish each of the following sentences in such a way that it means exactly the same as the sentence printed before it.

Example: He walked so slowly that he missed the bus.
If *he hadn't walked so slowly, he wouldn't have missed the bus.*

1 The picnic was cancelled because it rained.
If ______________________________

2 Without his father's help, he wouldn't have got that job.
If ______________________________

3 The car crashed because it was travelling too fast.
If ______________________________

4 I couldn't phone you because I'd lost your number.
If ______________________________

5 John caught a cold because he didn't wear a coat.
If ______________________________

6 He found the treasure as he was digging in his garden.
If ______________________________

7 I only knew about her wedding because I met her mother in the street.
If ______________________________

8 I lost my key so I had to wait outside in the snow.
If ______________________________

READING

1 *Stomach-ache* is often a symptom of food-poisoning. What other parts of the body can ache?

2 Look at these symptoms. Can you diagnose this illness? Use a dictionary to help you.

sore throat	sneezing	runny nose
aching limbs	coughing	shivering

1 What is the cure for this illness?
2 What can you do to relieve the symptoms?
3 What can you do to prevent yourself getting this type of illness?
4 Are these good ideas for getting rid of a cold?
- take a warm shower and a cold shower at regular intervals
- hold your face over a bowl of steam
- take very large doses of vitamin C
- eat lots of garlic
- eat nothing for 48 hours

3 Read this article quickly to find out:

1 Which of the ideas in the previous list is described.
2 What these numbers from the text refer to.

50	36–40	18–24	12–18
35	46	23	100

BUILD UP *with a cold spray*

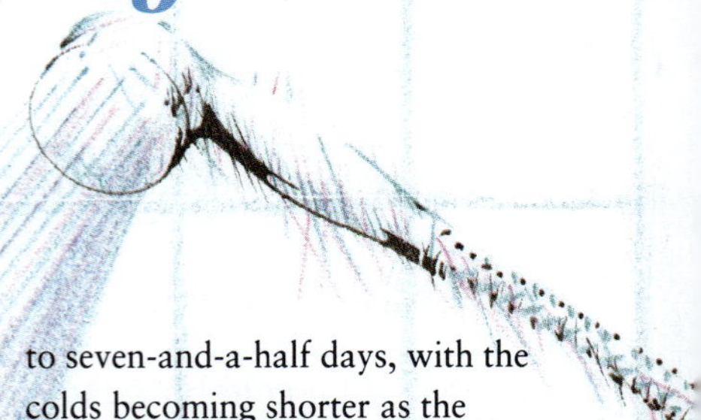

1 Cold showers are not everybody's favourite way to start the day, but even a half-hearted attempt, using a cold spray on your arms and legs, will help stave off a cold.

2 Researchers at Munich university medical school took 50 men and women aged between 20 and 50, divided them into two similar groups, and taught one group a simple hydrotherapy method to use at home five times per week. This was their schedule:

3 *Week 1*: Arms and legs only, five-minute warm shower (36–40°C) followed by 30-second cold shower (18–24°C). Repeated twice.

4 *Week 2*: Five-minute whole body warm shower followed by 30-second cold shower (same temperatures as above)

5 *Week 3 – Week 26*: Five-minute whole body warm shower followed by 30-second cold shower (12–18°C), with the cold shower being gradually lengthened to two minutes over the following two to three weeks.

6 The second group was given no instructions and were only monitored as to their incidence of colds. The results were exciting.

7 It was expected that, on average, everybody would have two colds during the six months of the study (50 colds in each group of 25 people). What actually happened was that the hydrotherapy group had only 35 colds, while the non-hydrotherapy group had 46. And when the six-month time scale was divided into two, an even more significant discovery emerged.

8 During the first three months the hydrotherapy group had 25 colds, compared with 23 in the other group. But during the second three months the hydrotherapists had only ten, while there were 23 colds in the untreated group. This clearly shows that there is a "hardening" effect from this method which builds up slowly and is really evident after three months of regular use.

9 Severity of the colds was also reduced among those having regular hot and cold showers, with the average length of their colds being just under six days, compared to seven-and-a-half days, with the colds becoming shorter as the treatment programme progressed.

10 Prof Ernst Edzard, the chief researcher, believes that, "An efficient, practical and inexpensive prophylaxis agianst one of the most frequent and expensive diseases in man has been identified at last." (Physiotherapy, April 1990).

11 The fact that this same method has been advocated by naturopaths for 100 years should not be forgotten in the euphoria of this medical "discovery". But now we have objective proof that we can increase our hardiness and reduce our susceptibility. You can help even more by regular vigorous "skin-brushing" using a damp towel, a light brush or a loofah. This will stimulate the skin and its amazing eliminative function, as well as help to improve overall circulatory efficiency.

4 Read more carefully and decide if these statements are true or false.

	True	False
1 The two groups are of equal size.		
2 The length of the warm shower was gradually reduced.		
3 The second group took only warm showers.		
4 Over six months the hydrotherapy group had fewer colds.		
5 Over the first three months the two groups had about the same number of colds.		
6 The non-hydrotherapy group had more severe and longer colds.		
7 The Munich research took place over 100 years ago.		
8 Damp towels are a common cause of colds.		

5 Find words in the text which mean

1 not very enthusiastic (paragraph 1)
2 protect yourself from (1)
3 timetable (2)
4 made longer (5)
5 checked (6)
6 how many times it happens (6)
7 important (7)
8 making harder (8)

6 Complete this table with the correct word.

Adjective	Noun	Verb
long	length	
	hardness	
wide		to widen
	depth	to deepen
	height	to heighten
fresh		
large		to enlarge
		to strengthen
weak		
		to soften
	darkness	
bright		

③

SPEAKING

1 Look at the three photographs below.

①

②

1 In a group of 3, each describe one of the photographs in detail.
2 Say how good each type of exercise is as a way of keeping fit.
3 Read this passage and decide which of the photographs it is talking about.

Behind closed doors, Britain's overworked and overweight are paying small fortunes to keep themselves in shape. The health and fitness trade is witnessing a surge in demand for personal trainers, who provide one-to-one tuition in body maintainance for fees of up to £45 an hour.

4 What are the advantages of having a personal trainer?
5 Is it worth the money?

2 Discuss with a partner how effective each of these activities is as a way of keeping fit and healthy:

	very effective	*quite effective*	*not very effective*
jogging			
cycling			
walking to work/school			
eating less			
a high-fibre diet			
playing a sport regularly			
sleeping late			
not smoking and drinking			
living in the country			

Which would be more suitable for

children?
parents?
grandparents?

3 Choose one of the following composition titles.

1 Young people should not be allowed to watch films which contain scenes of violence. Do you agree?

2 A young friend has recently been given a bicycle as a present. Write what you would say to your friend to explain some important aspects of road safety for cyclists.

3 What are some of the best ways in which people can keep fit and healthy in modern society?

4 Find a partner/partners who has/have chosen the same title. Together make a list of points and write a plan in the grid below.

1 ______________________________

2 ______________________________

3 ______________________________

4 ______________________________

5 ______________________________

You are now ready to write your composition. Write between 120 and 180 words in 45 minutes.

REVISION TEST 9

1 Finish each of the following sentences in such a way that it means exactly the same as the sentence printed before it.

Example: I haven't laughed so much for years.
It's years *since I laughed so much*.

1 The weather was so nice that they decided to eat outside.
It was such ______________________________

2 The house was so far from the road that you couldn't hear any traffic.
The house was such ______________________________

3 It was such a boring film that they left during the interval.
The film ______________________________

4 Although he had a bad cold, he went to work.
In spite ______________________________

5 I'm sunburnt because I didn't use any sunscreen.
I wish ______________________________

6 I caught a cold because I went out without a coat.
If I ______________________________

7 What a pity you didn't come to my party!
I wish ______________________________

8 I regret not finishing my homework at the weekend.
I wish ______________________________

9 Ronald ate too much and then felt sick.
If Ronald ______________________________

10 The train crash was the result of an electrical fault.
An electrical fault ______________________________

2 For each question 1–8 you must choose the word or phrase that best completes the sentence.

1 You should go to your dentist every year for a ________.
A check round **B** check over **C** check through **D** check up

2 Coffee has a wonderful ________.
A smell **B** perfume **C** scent **D** odour

3 She was complaining ________ a stomach-ache.
A by **B** from **C** over **D** of

4 It is dangerous ________ a plug with wet hands.
A to touch **B** to contact **C** to pull **D** to put

5 ________ the weather forecast it's going to be a sunny day.
A On account of **B** Owing to **C** As far as **D** According to

6 After a tiring day she enjoyed a hot ________ bath.
A relax **B** relaxation **C** relaxing **D** relaxed

7 The therapy had a good ________ on the patients.
A result **B** remedy **C** benefit **D** effect

8 There is an ________ kettle in your room for tea-making.
A electrical **B** electric **C** electricity **D** electrified

3 Complete each of the following sentences with the appropriate form of the word CATCH or with an expression formed from the word CATCH.

Example: If you are absent from class you are expected to *catch up* with the work in your own time.

1 I'm afraid I've ________ your cold.
2 He risked not ________ the train by leaving home at the last moment.
3 The Walkman was introduced in 1979 and ________ ________ very quickly.
4 She tried to explain but he wasn't able to ________ her meaning.
5 Although she got off to a slow start in the race, Jones soon began to ________ ________ ________ the other runners.

4 The word in capitals at the end of each of the following sentences can be used to form a word which fits suitably in the blank space. Fill each blank in this way.

Example: Please *ensure* that your seatbelts are securely fastened.	SURE
1 After taking some aspirin her headache ________	APPEAR
2 In Britain there is an enormous market for ________ pizzas.	FREEZE
3 A mechanical ________ caused the delay.	BREAK
4 As I like good food, I decided to go to ________ classes.	COOK
5 My new trousers are too long, they need ________	SHORT

5 Fill each of the numbered blanks in the following passage. Use only *one* word in each space.

At 34 years of ________ (1), Graham Simpson, the Foxton United captain, ________ (2) just led his team to the Second Division championship. Now, one year away ________ (3) retirement, he is a model ________ (4) fitness. He explains his enduring success ________ (5) pointing to a healthy lifestyle. He is still the ________ (6) weight as he was ten years ________ (7) and still as fast.

________ (8) many highly trained athletes, Graham likes to get ________ (9) least nine hours sleep a night, plus a regular couple of hours in the afternoon.

Graham is also careful ________ (10) his diet. He likes to eat food that gives a lot of energy but which is low ________ (11) fat. He ________ (12) eats a lot of bananas and tuna fish and has ________ (13) up fish and chips.

Graham ________ (14) to retire from football next year, but he is not likely to be collecting his old age pension ________ (15) yet!

UNIT 10 SALES TALK

VOCABULARY

1 Look at this picture and describe it to your partner. The following questions will help you.

1. What type of shop is this?
2. What are the people doing?
3. What things can you buy in this type of shop?
4. How is it organised?
5. What would you expect to find on the ground floor? in the basement? on the first floor? on the top floor?

2 You plan to visit Selfridges, a shop like the one in the picture. Here is your shopping list. All of the items can be found in six departments. Divide the items into six groups of five according to which department they can be found in. Give each department a name. The first one has been done for you.

Shopping List

ink	saucepan	rubber
plug	kettle	shampoo
bracelet	light bulb	brooch
necklace	smoked salmon	ruler
teaspoons	shaving foam	garlic
corkscrew	headphones	adaptor
earrings	pepper mill	toothpaste
batteries	mushrooms	sponge
envelopes	pencil sharpener	watch
bath foam	jam	peanuts

FOOD HALL	

3

trolley	checkout	cashier
till	carrier bag	aisle

1 Name as many things in the picture as you can. Begin with the words in the box.

2 What are the advantages and disadvantages of shopping in this type of place?

3 Think of some things you *have to do/need to do* in this type of shop compared to other types.

Think of some things you *needn't do/ don't have to do.*

READING

Look at the leaflet from Tesco, a large supermarket.

WHAT IS MULTISAVER?

Multisaver is the convenient way to make savings on your everyday shopping.

Throughout this store you'll see Multisaver signs on dozens of essential items and some of your favourite luxury goods as well. Offers will apply to single items or groups of products.

Simply buy the number of items shown on the Multisaver sign and you will automatically receive the discount indicated.

MULTI SAVER

Discounts are automatically deducted from your bill by our scanning system – even if the Multisaver items are spread throughout your shopping, provided they are purchased at the same time.

The savings you make will be shown both on the till screen and your receipt, indicated by the word "Multisaver" and a negative value.

THE MULTISAVER SIGN

BUITONI ITALIAN TAGLIATELLE 79p each 500 gram	MULTI SAVER 2 for £1.28 12.8p per 100 gram	BUY 2 SAVE 30p
The name of the product or range of products which qualify for the Multisaver offer	The number you need to buy	The discount you will receive

QUESTIONS AND ANSWERS

Q Do I need to purchase all of the items on the same trip?

A Yes. All items must be purchased in a single transaction.

Q Do I need to put the items together at the checkout?

A No. The discount will be deducted from your bill even if the Multisaver items are spread throughout your shopping. If the offer is "BUY 3 SAVE 10p". the discount will be shown after the 3rd item on your receipt.

Q If the offer is "BUY 3 SAVE 10p" and I buy 6, what will happen?

A You will qualify for the discount twice ie. 20p will be deducted. Any exception to this will be described on the Multisaver sign.

Q How will I know that I have received the discount?

A The savings you make will be shown both on the the till screen and on your receipt.

1 For each phrase decide whether this is something you *have to do* or *don't have to do* according to the leaflet, if you want to take advantage of Multisaver.

1 keep the discounted items separate
2 buy exactly the number printed on the sign
3 buy at least the number printed on the sign
4 tell the cashier you have discounted items in your shopping
5 take your receipt to a special desk
6 buy all the items on the same visit to the shop
7 show this leaflet to the cashier
8 go to a special Multisaver cashier
9 buy items that have a Multisaver sign on them
10 buy a particular product or range of products

2 Find words from the leaflet that mean

a easy and comfortable	f shown
b in all parts	g taken away
c necessary	h distributed
d also	i as long as
e individual	j bought

GRAMMAR

GR p184

Obligation

1 **1** For each of the expressions on the left choose the phrase on the right which means the same thing.

You need to go	It is necessary for you to go
You have to go	It is possible for you to go if you like
You must go	It would be better if you went
You can go	You have no choice but to go
You should go	

2 Which two phrases on the left mean the same thing?

3 For each of the expressions on the left choose the phrase on the right which means the same thing.

You don't have to go	It isn't necessary for you to go
You needn't go	It isn't possible for you to go
You don't need to go	It would be better not to go
You can't go	It is forbidden!
You shouldn't go	
You mustn't go	

4 Which three phrases on the left all mean the same thing?

2 Complete these sentences about supermarkets with one of the words or phrases from the box.

have to	don't have to	need to	can	should	can't	must
mustn't	needn't	shouldn't	don't need to			

1 You ________ push your own trolley.
2 You ________ change the price labels on the goods.
3 You ________ use a basket or trolley.
4 You ________ choose your own vegetables.
5 You ________ put things straight into your shopping bag.
6 You ________ push in front of people in the queue
7 You ________ sit down while the assistant finds things for you.
8 You ________ bring boxes and bags to take your goods home
9 You ________ compare prices with other supermarkets.
10 You ________ queue up at busy periods.
11 You ________ buy large quantities, and if you do you ________ go shopping so often.
12 You ________ allow children to eat the food before you reach the checkout.

SPEAKING

1 Choose one of the photographs and describe it to your partner. Use some of the expressions in the box.

on the right/left/in the centre		in the background/foreground
in the top left-hand corner		
in the bottom right-hand corner		
at the bottom	at the top	
it could be	it must be	
it might be	it can't be	it may be

2 Match two of the following passages to the photographs.

A **I like it because you can have a good look round and take your time without being bothered or talked into anything. You can try things on without feeling you have to buy them afterwards.**

B **You needn't go to London for style and exclusivity. We can offer that something special, a really personal service. Our trained and experienced staff are on hand to advise you on the perfect outfit for every occasion.**

C **Price is our main advantage, of course. People come here because they know they can get the same stuff cheaper. We don't have to pay high rents, heating bills or anything like that, so our prices are lower.**

3 Which of these places is best for buying clothes? Give reasons. Decide the good and the bad points about each place.

①

②

LISTENING 1

Listen to the conversation and decide whether these statements are true or false.

1 Anne thinks Liz's top was expensive.
2 You are not allowed to try clothes on in the shop.
3 If you bring them back you can exchange them for other goods.
4 To get a refund you have to prove the clothes do not fit.
5 The shop only accepts payments in cash.
6 Ferguson clothes are only sold in Ferguson's.
7 Liz persuades Anne to go to the shop.
8 Anyone can have a Ferguson's card.

GRAMMAR GR p184
Make/let/allow

1 Look at these phrases from the listening text.

they make you pay in cash
they don't let you try things on
you're allowed to pay it off
you're not allowed to try things on

When do we use *make*, *let* and *allow*?

2 Put the correct form of *make*, *let* or *allow* in the spaces in these sentences.

1 Oh, I hate piano recitals. Please don't ________ me go.
2 You're not ________ to eat or drink in the computer room.
3 When I was young, I was ________ to wear horrible long woollen socks.
4 Her father is strict, he won't ________ her wear make-up.
5 He is not ________ to go out after nine o'clock in the evening.
6 They ________ that dog climb all over people who visit them.
7 At that school they don't ________ the students wear high-heeled shoes.
8 I wasn't ________ to go to a pop concert until I was sixteen.

3 Discuss these questions with your partner:

1 Should people be allowed to choose their own birthday presents?
2 Should parents let their teenage children smoke at home?
3 Should all teenagers be made to have a bank account?
4 Should children be made to help with the housework?
5 Should parents let children buy whatever clothes they want?

READING

1 Do you recognise this character? What do you know about it?

Just potty about Paddington

by GRAHAM LORD

THIRTY years ago this week a little children's book was published that was to launch its hero into international stardom and to make its author very rich indeed.

A Bear Called Paddington marked the birth, in 1958, of a huge business that today includes Paddington books, toys and 700 worldwide products, from clothes and games to pots of marmalade.

The **scruffy** accident-prone little bear from Darkest Peru has inspired a frenzy of radio and TV programmes, stage plays, films, and even a musical — and American and Japanese fans have been known to pay for extra airline seats to fly giant Paddingtons home.

CREATOR

Now there's even a Paddington biography, THE LIFE AND TIMES OF PADDINGTON BEAR (Pavilion, £12.95) by Russell Ash and Paddington's creator, Michael Bond.

The Japanese are especially **potty** about Paddington and he even appears on the Mitsui Bank's credit cards.

His appeal crosses every frontier, age group and class from Twiggy to the Royals. Ice-skater Jayne Torvill has three mini-Paddingtons on her sports bag, and even Mrs Thatcher waved a blue-rosetted Paddington **aloft** at the Tory conference in 1978.

Richard Branson carried a Paddington on his record-breaking transatlantic crossing in Virgin Atlantic. So did the Oxford University expedition to Darkest Peru — and complaining children forced British Rail to install a 45-inch Paddington in a glass case at Paddington Station.

When Michael Bond was inspired to write that first story he never dreamed of the fame and furore to come.

A BBC TV cameraman who lived with his wife, Brenda, in a one-room flat in London, he missed his bus in Oxford Street on Christmas Eve, 1956, and **wandered** into Selfridges to escape the rain.

On a shelf in the toy department he **spotted** one last, lonely, unsold bear "looking rather sorry for himself."

He took it home, called it Paddington after the nearby station, **kitted it out** with a duffle coat and tiny suitcase and eventually **scribbled** a little story about a bear arriving at Paddington Station with a label reading: 'PLEASE LOOK AFTER THIS BEAR. THANK YOU.'

No fewer than seven publishers rejected the book. But Collins bought it for £75 — and the rest is legend.

Since then the Paddington books have sold more than 20 million copies and Michael Bond still has the original lonely bear that started it all.

STRESS

Sadly, Bond's huge **merchandising** success destroyed his marriage. He was soon working a 16-hour day and relying on pills and **booze** to keep going, and the stress drove the Bonds to divorce.

But he says that he and his ex-wife remain good friends, thanks to Paddington, and the bear has brought him a lot of fun and laughter.

Best of all are the thousands of letters that arrive each year from all over the world.

"Keep on writing those books!" wrote one girl. "Maybe you will become famous."

"Are you related to James Bond?" asked another child.

Most **flattering** of all was the note from a boy who said: "Now I have come to think of Paddington as a bear, it seems a funny name for a station."

With your partner decide who is Student A and who is Student B. Read the article quickly. Find and underline each of the names on your list and say why it is important to the article.

Student A: Paddington Station
Peru
Japan
Oxford
Oxford Street
Selfridges

Student B: Michael Bond
Mrs Thatcher
Richard Branson
Twiggy
James Bond
Jayne Torvill

Tell your partner what you have found.

2 Together, put the following events mentioned in the article into the order in which they happened in real life.

a Paddington appears in 700 products worldwide.
b He gave the bear a duffle coat and a suitcase.
c It was raining.
d Collins agreed to publish the story.
e He wrote a story about the bear.
f Michael Bond bought a bear in Selfridges.
g The Bonds' marriage broke up.
h The story was a great success.

3 Write a paragraph linking the events together into a narrative. Use at least four of the words and expressions in the box.

which	where	when	but	later
however	so	after	that	then

Start your paragraph like this:

It all began on a wet Christmas Eve in 1956

____
____
____

4 Match each of the words from the text on the left with a suitable equivalent from the list on the right. The words are in bold type in the article. Look at the context to help you.

scruffy	equipped
potty	above the head
aloft	walked aimlessly
wandered	alcoholic drink
spotted	untidy
kitted out	marketing
scribbled	enthusiastic
merchandising	wrote quickly
booze	saying nice things
flattering	noticed

LISTENING 2

1 Look at this dialogue.

With your partner try to decide what the customer says.
Read all the dialogue before you begin.
Write your ideas on line **a**.

Shop Assistant: Good morning. Can I help you?
1 Customer: a ______
b ______

Shop Assistant: Did you have any particular colour in mind?
2 Customer: a ______
b ______

Shop Assistant: Dark blue or light blue?
3 Customer: a ______
b ______

Shop Assistant: Yes, we have. This one comes in both long-sleeved and sleeveless styles.
4 Customer: a ______
b ______

Shop Assistant: No, actually it's 50% wool and 50% acrylic.
5 Customer: a ______
b ______

Shop Assistant: Yes, we have, but not in dark blue, only in light.
6 Customer: a ______
b ______

Shop Assistant: It's £29.99.
7 Customer: a ______
b ______

Shop Assistant: Yes, of course. What size do you take?
8 Customer: a ______
b ______

Shop Assistant: OK. Here you are. The fitting room is at the back of the shop on the left.
9 Customer: a ______
b ______

2 Now listen to Part 1 and on line **b** write down what the customer really says. One of you should listen for the *red* lines and one for the *blue* lines.Does the customer say what you wrote in **a**? If not, is your version acceptable?

3 Now look at this dialogue. Complete line **a** as before.

1 Shop Assistant: a ______
b ______
Customer: Yes, I'm looking for a T-shirt.

2 Shop Assistant: a ______
b ______
Customer: Well, green I suppose. It should match these trousers I'm wearing.

3 Shop Assistant: a ______
b ______
Customer: Oh no, I don't like that. I'd prefer a plain one if you've got it.

4 Shop Assistant: a ______
b ______
Customer: It doesn't matter. The colour's more important.

5 Shop Assistant: a ______
b ______
Customer: Yes, that's a good match. Is it 100% cotton?

6 Shop Assistant: a ______
b ______
Customer: Good. And how much does it cost?

7 Shop Assistant: a ______
b ______
Customer: In that case I'll take the short-sleeved one, please.

8 Shop Assistant: a ______
b ______
Customer: Medium, please.

9 Shop Assistant: a ______
b ______
Customer: By credit card, please.

10 Shop Assistant: a ______
b ______

4 Now listen to Part 2 to check.

VOCABULARY

1 Read this story and choose a word from the box to fit into each of the numbered blanks.

instalments	bill	sale	discount
deposit	currency	cost	afford
buy	cash	exchange	bargain
price	debt	worth	spending
pay	wallet	bank	~~receipt~~

Bruce walked out of the travel agency and looked at the (1) *receipt* he had been given. It had been so easy to book the holiday in the Caribbean. The assistant had been very helpful and persuasive. He had been attracted by the 25% (2) _______ offered on the (3) _______ in the brochure if you booked before the end of the month. He had only had to pay a (4) _______ of £100 to be followed by four monthly (5) _______ of £75, surely he could (6) _______ that?

He realised, however, that he had forgotten to ask about the (7) _______ of living on the island or about the (8) _______ rate of the local (9) _______ . These were important because he had only booked bed and breakfast and so would have to (10) _______ other meals out of his (11) _______ money.

He took his (12) _______ from his pocket and remembered that he had to go to the (13) _______ because he had run out of (14) _______ . Oh dear, and there inside was the electricity (15) _______ that he had forgotten to (16) _______ .

He stopped and looked up. He was outside a very smart clothes shop. In the window there was a big sign with (17) '_______' written on it and there next to it was a lovely lightweight jacket. It would be just the thing for the Caribbean, and at only £55 it was a real (18) _______ . Even if it meant going into (19) _______ , he couldn't resist such a good chance to save money. He walked into the shop. 'This holiday had better be (20) _______ it,' he said to himself.

2 Now choose the best answer to each question.

1 What did Bruce have to do in order to get a discount?
- A Go on holiday before the end of the month.
- B Agree to have bed and breakfast only.
- C Pay the rest of the money by the end of the month.
- D Pay the deposit now and more money later.

2 How did Bruce feel after he left the travel agency?
- A He wished he'd been to the bank.
- B He wished he'd booked more meals.
- C He wished he'd asked more questions.
- D He wished he'd changed some currency.

3 Why did Bruce decide to buy the jacket?
- A The shop was very smart.
- B He had some money to spend.
- C It had been reduced in price.
- D He needed it for his holidays.

4 Which of these sentences best describes Bruce?
- A He thinks carefully before buying things.
- B He is rich and extravagant.
- C He often regrets spending too much money.
- D He is often persuaded to buy things.

3 Choose the best word A, B, C or D to complete each sentence.

1 The assistant ________ Bruce to book the holiday.
A suggested B persuaded C made D let

2 The holiday seemed to be good ________ for money.
A worth B bargain C value D use

3 She paid for the shoes by ________ .
A cash B instalments C credit D cheque

4 Bruce regretted not ________ about the cost of living.
A asking B asked C ask D have asked

LISTENING 3

1 Listen to the phone-in programme and make notes under these headings.

	Name	Wish	Reason
1st caller			
2nd caller			
3rd caller			
4th caller			

2 Compare your notes with your partner, then listen again to check.

3 Look at these sentences from the listening and answer the questions.

1 I wish I could ski.
a Can she ski?
b How does she feel about it?

2 I wish I was rich.
a Is she rich?
b How does she feel about it?

4 Listen again and make a note of four other sentences using *I wish*.

How many different types of sentence are there? How are they different?
Ask yourself questions as in the example.

GRAMMAR GR p184
Wishes

1 Match **eight** of the sentences **1 – 10** with one of the phrases **a – h** to show the meaning. Note that there are two sentences which cannot be matched.

1 I wish I could ski.
2 I wish you luck.
3 I wish I knew what . to buy
4 I wish I had blonde hair.
5 I wish I was rich.
6 I wish they'd be quiet.
7 I wish you a happy birthday.
8 I wish you could come with me.
9 I wish he didn't always sing in the bath.
10 I wish I had asked more questions.

a But I'm not.
b But I don't.
c But I didn't.
d But I can't.
e But I haven't.
f But they won't.
g But he does.
h But you can't.

2 Which two sentences from 1 - 10 cannot be matched? Why? What other things can you wish people in this way?

Which of the sentences 1 – 10 expresses past regrets (studied in Unit 9)?

3 Is there anything about yourself or other people you would like to change?

Somewhere in the room there is a magic crystal which can grant three wishes.

Finish the sentences below with your wishes.

1 I wish I was ________
2 I wish I could ________
3 I wish I had ________
4 I wish ________ would ________
5 I wish ________ could ________

4 Now tell your wishes to as many people in the room as possible.

When you have found someone with the same wish as you, you have found the magic crystal and your wish can be granted. Only the first three wishes count, so don't waste any time.

5 Complete each of the following sentences in such a way that it means exactly the same as the sentence printed before it.

Example: It's a shame that I can't drive.
I wish *I could drive*.

1 I'm sorry that you can't come to the party.
I wish ______________________________

2 He keeps interrupting me, which is very annoying.
I wish ______________________________

3 Ingrid would like to be able to swim, but she can't.
Ingrid wishes ______________________________

4 I hope that you are lucky in your exams.
I wish you ______________________________

5 My hair's short and dark, but I'd prefer long blonde hair.
I wish I ______________________________

6 Eric doesn't see his grandchildren very often, which makes him sad.
Eric wishes ______________________________

7 I'm sorry that he won't accept the job he's been offered.
I wish he ______________________________

8 I have very little patience, which is a shame!
I wish ______________________________

9 This continual rain is making me feel depressed.
I wish it ______________________________

10 The print in this book is so small that I'm afraid I can't read it.
I wish the ______________________________

WRITING

1 Read the letter on the next page written by somebody who went on the coach trip advertised above.

Why has it been written?

25 Lowton Street
Milton
ML3 8PY

22 December

The Manager
Happycoaches Ltd
Milton
ML1 6WP

Sir or Madam,

I am writing to complain about a Happycoaches day trip which I went on to the Newton Stilton shopping complex on December 19th 1993.

According to your leaflet, the coach was supposed to leave at 8.30 in the morning. I arrived at 8.20 to find no coach waiting, and it did not arrive until after 9.00. **To make matters worse**, when eventually we left, the coach went at such speed along the country lanes that I felt nervous and uncomfortable (although the journey still took nearly three hours). Is there not a more direct route?

As if this were not enough, when we finally arrived at Newton Stilton I found that the new shopping complex was half closed. Many of the best shops will not be opening until the spring. I am afraid that your leaflet is rather misleading in this respect.

On top of everything, the coach broke down on the return journey and we had to wait for an hour before another coach was sent.

You can imagine how disappointed I am to have wasted a day in this way, and I feel that your company is directly to blame. I am, therefore, writing to request an immediate refund of the £9.50 I spent on the ticket.

I look forward to receiving your prompt reply.

Yours faithfully,

D. Stanton

2 Give each paragraph in the letter a title.

1 Introduction
2
3
4
5

3 Look at the phrases which are in bold type. How are they important to the letter?

4 Look at these informal expressions. For each one find the formal equivalent in the letter.

1 your leaflet says
2 it doesn't tell the truth about this
3 I'm really fed up about it
4 it's your fault
5 so I want my money back
6 write back soon

LISTENING 4

1 Listen to a man making a complaint in a shop and make notes under the following headings.

1 What did he buy?
2 What is his complaint?
3 What happened as a result?
4 Why did it happen
- according to the assistant?
- according to the customer?

5 What exactly does the customer want?
6 Why is this not possible?
7 What does he decide to do?
8 What else will he complain about?

2 Listen again and then plan the paragraphs of the letter the customer will write to the manager.

3 Now write the letter. Use the letter above as a model.

REVISION TEST 10

1 For each question 1–10 you must choose the word or phrase that best completes the sentence.

1 I wish you _______ stop correcting every word I say.
A should **B** had **C** would **D** will

2 The company went bankrupt due to _______ of investment.
A insufficient **B** lack **C** scarce **D** drought

3 Her mother wouldn't _______ her ride a bicycle.
A allow **B** permit **C** let **D** accept

4 How much did you pay _______ that coat?
A to **B** for **C** from **D** at

5 When travelling between England and Scotland, you _______ carry a passport.
A shouldn't **B** mustn't **C** can't **D** needn't

6 She _______ a new kitchen table from a mail-order catalogue.
A booked **B** applied for **C** wrote **D** ordered

7 _______ you try these trousers on, you can't be sure they'll fit.
A Provided **B** Unless **C** Whether **D** As long as

8 Take some warm clothes _______ it gets cold in the evening.
A provided **B** owing to **C** in case **D** so that

9 If only I _______ agreed to go on such an expensive holiday!
A hadn't **B** didn't **C** haven't **D** wasn't

10 After waiting an hour he realised the bus was _______ to come.
A improbable **B** uncertain **C** impossible **D** unlikely

2 Complete each of the following sentences with a phrasal verb that includes the word PUT.

Example: The day was so warm he decided to put <u>on</u> a T-shirt.

1 The children put their toys _______ before they went to bed.

2 Please put the books _______ on the correct shelf when you have finished reading them.

3 Ray has put _______ _______ a new job. I hope he gets it.

4 The party has been put _______ until next week due to heavy snowfalls.

5 I'm determined to do it, and nothing you can say will put me _______ .

6 He has put _______ a lot of weight during the holiday.

7 Some shops near the beach put their prices _______ in the tourist season.

3 Fill each of the blanks with one suitable word which is connected with the subject of MONEY.

Example: I'm sorry, I've only got a £10 note. Could you *change* it?

1 What is the exchange ________ for the Australian dollar, please?

2 She put her money into a bank account that paid 8% ________ .

3 If you buy five items, you'll receive a 10% ________ at the till.

4 Could I pay by cheque, please? I don't have quite enough money with me to pay in ________ .

5 Because their value increases quickly, works of art and antiques make a very good ________ .

4 Below are five groups of three words. In the space write a word which describes each group.

Example: shoes, boots, sandals *footwear*

1 plates, cups, saucers ________

2 soap, shampoo, toothpaste ________

3 earring, necklace, bracelet ________

4 van, coach, car ________

5 envelope, ruler, rubber ________

5 You will hear a series of announcements made to customers in a department store. As you listen, complete the information in the grid below.

Department	**Product**	**Offer**	**Floor**
Food Hall	bread	Reduced	1.
2.	soft furnishings	20% off	3.
4.	Brighthouse Cleaning Products	5.	basement
Restaurant	6.	set meal £3.20	7.
8.	The Miltons by J. Bakerson	signed copy	9.
10.	suits	11.	12.

UNIT 11

ENVIRONMENTALLY YOURS

SPEAKING

1 Look at this photograph and discuss the following points. Give reasons for your opinions.

1 The picture in general:
Where was the picture taken?
What time of year or day is it?
How are the people dressed?
How do they feel?
How do they feel about each other?

2 Looking beyond the picture:
What has just happened?
What have the people been doing?
What is going to happen?
What are the people going to do?

3 Extending the theme:
What is the main character doing?
Is it a good idea? Why?
How would you feel in this situation?
Could this happen in your town?

2 Decide which of these three passages best matches this picture. Say why you think so.

A **The British Lung Foundation claims that the masks' long term health benefits are considerable. Newspaper vendor Stuart Crichton, who has spent five years inhaling exhaust fumes at Covent Garden tube station said "It's a good idea – the air's vile. When it's hot and muggy you can hardly breathe."**

B **People avoided my gaze as I walked through London's Covent Garden. There wasn't much point in smiling back. After an hour I was desperate to take it off because I felt ridiculous. After two hours, I felt vaguely sick. Frankly, I can't see them catching on.**

C **The Clean Air Act of 1956 that followed the deaths of 4000 people due to a London pea-souper smog has almost wiped out emissions of deadly Sulphur Dioxide. But concern is mounting over invisible 'ozone smog', a poisonous cocktail created when car fumes such as Nitrogen Dioxide and Carbon Monoxide are heated by sunlight.**

3 Discuss the advantages and disadvantages of each of the following solutions to the problem of air pollution. Think about a big city in your country, or a city like London or Los Angeles.

1 Increase tax on petrol.
2 Limit each family to one car.
3 Close the city centre to traffic.
4 Improve the bus services.
5 Create special roads for bicycles.
6 Build underground railways.
7 Build bigger car parks.
8 Use electric cars.

READING

1 Read the article and underline the parts where these questions are answered:

1 What do the masks do?
2 Who is already using them?
3 Who should be wearing them?
4 What does the BLF predict?
5 Who is thinking about using masks?
6 Who doesn't the mask work for?
7 Who thinks the mask is not the solution?
8 What other solution is proposed?

Are you safe to go out without a smog mask?

by Cathy Scott-Clark

Pollution at danger levels, say experts

SMOG masks which filter toxic gases out of the air we breathe could soon be a common sight on city streets, air pollution experts say.

Space-age masks are already a frequent accessory for cyclists. But, with toxic ozone levels now rising at an alarming rate, experts say pedestrians should be wearing them too.

The Clean Air act of 1956 that followed the deaths of 4,000 people due to a London pea-soup smog has almost wiped out emissions of deadly sulphur dioxide.

But concern is mounting over invisible "ozone smog", a poisonous cocktail created when car fumes such as nitrogen dioxide and carbon monoxide are heated by sunlight.

Last week the British Lung Foundation (BLF) predicted that London could become as polluted as Los Angeles and Athens within 15 years.

Dr Malcolm Green, BLF chairman, said if the current pollution levels continued, all city dwellers, who were outside for 20 minutes or more, would have to wear masks. Traffic wardens,cyclists, messengers and transport police should be wearing them already, he warns, particularly those prone to chest infections, asthma or bronchitis.

"The reduction of air pollution must be our first priority, but this takes time. Masks are a sensible way of protecting lungs."

A Metropolitan Police spokeswoman confirmed that smog masks for officers and traffic wardens in London are now being considered.

But Liz Marriot of the London Cycles Campaign says their use is limited.

"Unless a mask makes a perfect seal on your face, it doesn't work. Where does that leave men with beards, people who wear glasses or someone with a big nose?'

Curbed

Friends of the Earth air pollution experts say wearing of masks is not a long-term solution.

"Nobody wants a world in which people have to wear masks in the street," says campaigner Fiona Weir.

"This is a new generation of pollution. Numbers of vehicles are constantly rising and ozone pollution is rising very, very rapidly — car usage has to be curbed."

Government success at ending the Fifties pea-soupers has led to complacency at the growing danger of toxic vehicle fumes which make up ozone, she claims.

FoE is concerned that toxic ozone levels in Britain now regularly exceed World Health Organisation safety guidelines.

2 Find words which mean:

1 poisonous (1)
2 frightening (9)
3 a mixture (20)
4 part of the body (organ) (24)
5 likely to suffer from (38)
6 most important thing (41)
7 where nothing can pass (53)
8 reduced (71)

3 For each of the following questions choose the best answer, A, B, C or D.

1 What does Dr Malcolm Green think?
A London has as much air pollution as Athens.
B Smog masks solve the problem of air pollution.
C People working outside should wear a mask in London.
D A mask is necessary after twenty minutes in London.

2 Why does Liz Marriot have doubts about the masks?
A They do not work so well for cyclists.
B The number of cars is always rising.
C The masks do not fit everyone perfectly.
D The masks do not work over a long time.

3 What do Friends of the Earth think?
A People cannot be forced to wear masks.
B World Health Organisation levels are too low.
C A new generation of cleaner vehicles is needed.
D People must use their cars less.

VOCABULARY

Put a preposition in each of the numbered spaces in the following passage.

Recently, the authorities (1) _______ Athens were forced (2) _______ ban all cars (3) _______ the city centre (4) _______ one day because (5) _______ the levels of air pollution.

Meanwhile, (6) _______ California, a law has been passed saying that no car manufacturer will be allowed (7) _______ sell cars (8) _______ the state after 1998, unless (9) _______ least two percent (10) _______ its sales are in Zero Emission Vehicles (ZEVs). This percentage will rise (11) _______ ten percent (12) _______ subsequent years.

The only true ZEVs are electrically-powered cars that run (13) _______ batteries and most car manufacturers are now working (14) _______ electric models.

Other U.S. states have followed California's example which suggests that the electric car may be the car (15) _______ the future.

WRITING

Choose one of these composition titles. Make a list of the main points you will want to mention.

1 What can be done to solve the problems of smog in large cities?
2 What are the advantages and disadvantages of wearing smog masks?
3 The only solution to the problem of urban smog is to limit the use of cars. Do you agree?

Compare your list with someone else in the class who has chosen the same title.

You are now ready to write your composition (120-180 words). Make your plan.

GRAMMAR *GR p185*

Reported Speech: Statements

1 In the pictures below decide which person is using each of the tenses in this list. Some people use more than one tense.

present simple	past simple
present continuous	past continuous
present perfect	
present perfect continuous	
'going to' future	

What happens to each of these tenses in reported speech?

2 Rewrite each of the sentences below, using reported speech, to show what each of the people in the pictures said.

Alice: I support Friends of the Earth and other environmental movements.

Andrew: I have been living in Athens for ten years and I've noticed the pollution getting worse.

Norman: I was living in London during the famous smogs of the nineteen fifties.

Jane: I was visiting Los Angles last year and was very surprised by levels of atmospheric pollution there.

Alan: I'm going to buy a car that uses unleaded petrol next time.

Liz: I'm organising a campaign in favour of banning cars from our city centre.

Sally: I have always supported the idea of using public transport instead of private cars.

3 Look at these reported statements about other things that each of the people in the pictures said. Try to decide what their actual words were.

Example: Alice said that she had raised a lot of money for environmental charities since 1990.
Alice said, *'I've raised a lot of money for environmental charities since 1990.'*

1 Norman said that London was much cleaner than it had been in 1960.
Norman said, '____________________
2 Andrew said that there were going to be further restrictions on traffic in Athens.
Andrew said, '____________________
3 Jane said that underground railways were being built in California.
Jane said, '____________________
4 Alan said he had been trying to use his car less.
Alan said, '____________________
5 Liz said that she had been using the bus every day for ten years.
Liz said, '____________________
6 Sally said she never used her car unless it was really necessary.
Sally said, '____________________

LISTENING 1

1 Listen to Part 1 and decide which of the speakers uses each of the following modal verbs.

	Bob	Lidia	Les
1 can			
2 may			
3 must			
4 will			

What happens to these verbs in reported speech?

Listen again and make a note of the main point each speaker makes.

Now write a sentence that summarises that main point in reported speech (use the four modal verbs above).

2 Listen to Part 2 and compare your sentences with the interviewer's.

3 Now listen to Part 3 and decide which speaker uses each of the following modal verbs.

	Gordon	Mary
1 should		
2 would		
3 could		
4 might		
5 ought to		

What happens to these verbs in reported speech?

Listen again and make a note of the main point each speaker makes.

Now write a sentence in reported speech summarising each main point using the verbs above.

4 Compare your sentences with your partner's.

GRAMMAR GR p185

Reported Speech: Time changes

What other words change in reported speech?

Example: 'I had a lovely surprise yesterday' said Karen.
Karen said *she had had a lovely surprise* | *the previous day.* / *the day before.*

Match the direct speech phrase or word on the left with its reported speech equivalent on the right.

1 yesterday	**a** then
2 tomorrow night	**b** three years previously
3 tonight	**c** the previous day
4 here	**d** that
5 now	**e** the following week
6 this	**f** the night before
7 next week	**g** that night
8 these	**h** there
9 last night	**i** those
10 three years ago	**j** the following night

LISTENING 2

1 What does *recycling* mean?
What materials are recycled?
What other things could be recycled?
What are the advantages and disadvantages of recycling?

2 Label the car using the words in the box.

bonnet boot bumper aeriel
windscreen dashboard sunroof
headlights number plate
rear-view mirror windscreen wiper

3 Listen and decide if the following statements are true or false:

1 The metal part of a car is already recyclable.
2 25% of a car is not made of metal.
3 Some new cars are made entirely of plastic.
4 Car bumpers usually get replaced after an accident.
5 The local garage makes new bumpers from the damaged plastic.
6 New plastic is put onto the old bumpers.
7 Most of the plastic from damaged bumpers is not used for new bumpers.
8 Drivers whose bumpers are recycled get new bumpers free.
9 Some recyclable car parts are very valuable.

4 What questions does Nick ask Jenny? Listen again and make a note of his questions.

5 How do we put questions into reported speech? Write in reported speech the five questions Nick asked Jenny.

Which one is different? Why is it different?

6 Finish each of the following sentences in such a way that it means exactly the same as the sentence printed before it.

1 'What time is it Frances?' said Tim.
Tim asked Frances ____________________
2 'Are you coming to the party tonight, Joanna?' said Adam.
Adam asked Joanna ____________________
3 'Can I borrow your pen please, Sam?' said Gillian.
Gillian asked Sam ____________________
4 'Do you know what's on at the cinema, James?' said Pamela.
Pamela asked James ____________________
5 'Have you finished your homework yet?' Robin said Sandra.
Robin asked Sandra ____________________
6 Julia asked Phil if he would look after her cat while she was on holiday.
Julia said, '____________________
7 Wendy asked me to get her some stamps from the post office.
Wendy said, '____________________
8 Caroline asked me what time the meeting would end.
Caroline said, '____________________
9 Helen asked the waiter for another spoon.
Helen said, '____________________
10 Mark asked Valerie if she had got a car.
Mark said, '____________________

7 In reported questions when can we use
1 if / whether?
2 an infinitive (e.g. to go)?
3 a question word (e.g. when)?

Look again at 1–5 in exercise 6. Can they be rewritten using alternative forms?

READING

1 What is happening to the Tropical rain forests?
Why is this a problem?
What can we do to help?

2 Match the words on the left with the definitions on the right. Use your dictionary if necessary.

timber	plants grown for food
species	wood used for making things
crops	something you buy
decade	a family of plants or animals
currently	a period of ten years
a purchase	at the moment

3 Read the article and circle:
a 3 words connected with water.
b 2 types of shop.
c 3 illnesses.
d 3 things made from wood.
e 3 industries.
f 3 ways in which people have been killed.

4 Read again and underline the verbs which are in the passive.

Why has the passive been used in each case?

5 Using the passive, write 3 sentences describing things that Friends of the Earth has achieved.

Why we must fight the destruction

When rainforests are cleared and burned millions of tonnes of carbon dioxide are released into the atmosphere affecting climatic conditions and threatening us all with severe flooding, drought and crop failure.

The rainforests contain at least half of the Earth's species. At the current rate of devastation an estimated 50 species worldwide become extinct every day.

One in four purchases from your chemists is derived from the rainforests. Scientists are currently caught in a race against time to find rainforest treatments for cancer, AIDS and heart disease – before they are lost forever.

Tribal people in the rainforests have been shot, poisoned and infected with disease to which they have no resistance – to make room for logging, mining and dams.

If this destruction continues only nine of the 33 countries currently exporting rainforest timber will have any left by the end of the decade.

Almost everyone will have part of the rainforests in their home, as DIY stores still supply and the construction industry still uses tropical hardwoods for doors, window frames and even toilet seats.

Please help us save the tropical rainforests now, before it's too late.

What Friends of the Earth has done

Friends of the Earth's Tropical Rainforest Campaign has been fighting to save the rainforests for six years. In that time, we've achieved a great deal.

- We've forced the British Government – and even timber trade organisations themselves – to acknowledge just how short-sighted the devastation is.
- We have persuaded major international companies to stop industrial activities that harm the rainforests.
- And by mobilising consumer pressure, we have helped reduce imports of tropical timber into the UK by nearly a third.

There's still a lot more to do. With your help, we can build on our success.

WRITING

1 Which of these photographs would make a good poster for Friends of the Earth to use in your country?

2 With your partner decide the good points and bad points of each picture as a way of encouraging people to give money to help the rain forests.

3 Make notes about the good and bad points of each picture.

4 Complete each of the following paragraphs to explain your choice.

I would choose picture number ________ because ________________________________
____

My second choice would be ______________
____
____

I certainly would not choose _____________
____
____

①

③

②

④

GRAMMAR *GR p186*

Impersonal Passive

1 **1** Look at these sentences. In what situation would the second sentence be more appropriate?

Friends of the Earth say that fifty species become extinct every day.

It is said that fifty species become extinct every day.

2 Look at the sentences in the box.

How certain are we about the information?
What is the source of the information?
What are the advantages of using this type of phrase?

> His wife is believed to be from the USA.
> She is understood to be very lonely.
> Emma is reported to be living in Africa.
> It is said that he cooks very well.
> It is thought that a cure for cancer may be found.

2 Rewrite each of the following sentences in such a way that it means exactly the same as the sentence printed before it.

1 People say that Lorna has many friends in London.
Lorna ______________________________

2 People think that he is living abroad.
He ______________________________

3 Graham is said to be very generous.
Everyone ______________________________

4 The world is believed to be getting warmer.
People ______________________________

5 Ronald is understood to be a supporter of Friends of the Earth.
I've heard ______________________________

LISTENING 3

1 Listen to eight short dialogues, and choose the sentence below which best summarises what is said.

1 A He warned me not to go near the dog.
B He advised me not to go near the dog.
C He persuaded me that I shouldn't go near the dog.

2 A He recommended the restaurant to me.
B He persuaded me to go to the restaurant.
C He invited me to go to the restaurant.

3 A He encouraged me to go in for the competition.
B He reminded me to go in for the competition.
C He told me to go in for the competition.

4 A He persuaded me to work harder.
B He told me to work harder.
C He advised me to work harder.

5 A He warned us to take our passports.
B He reminded us to take our passports.
C He advised us to take our passports.

6 A He offered her a cup of tea.
B She persuaded me to have a cup of tea.
C She reminded me to have a cup of tea.

7 A He admitted stealing the money.
B He denied stealing the money.
C He apologised for stealing the money.

8 A He promised to buy her a present.
B He offered to buy her a present.
C He refused to buy her a present.

2 What is the difference in meaning between these verbs?
A persuade/encourage
B advise/warn

3 Look again at the verbs used above in questions 1–8 and decide if they are type **A**, **B** or **C**, or a different type.

Type A verb + person + infinitive with 'to'
example: He asked me to go to the cinema.

Type B verb + infinitive with 'to'
example: She agreed to type the report.

Type C verb + 'ing'
example: He regretted dropping the vase.

LISTENING 4

You will hear a member of a college ecology society talking at a student meeting.

1 Listen and tick (✓) to show which of the things on the list she proposes.

- Stop using photocopied handouts ☐
- Recycling waste paper ☐
- Using plastic cups and plates ☐
- Better facilities for cyclists ☐
- Using paper bags instead of plastic ☐
- Not using products tested on animals ☐
- Changing cleaning materials ☐
- Recycling used batteries ☐
- Changing the central heating system ☐
- Providing more vegetarian menus ☐

2 Here is a report of the meeting which appeared in the college magazine. Unfortunately, it is not very accurate because the reporter was late for the meeting and missed the talk. He got the story from a friend who was there.

Listen to the talk again, and underline any incorrect information in the article.
As you can imagine, Tanya was not very pleased to read this. She decided to write to the magazine immediately to complain about the article, to correct the information and to ask for an apology.

At last week's meeting, Tanya Butler from the college ecology society made some dramatic proposals about how we should make the college more environmentally-friendly.

Ms Butler said that most of the handouts prepared by the teachers and photocopied for students were rubbish. She reported that most of them got thrown away and should be used to make recycled paper.

Ms Butler also claimed that a lot of paper was being wasted in the college office because the secretaries did not type on both sides of the paper. She suggested that they type on the back of old student worksheets instead!

Ms Butler went on to propose that the college cafeteria should serve only vegetarian meals and that students should wash up the plastic plates and cups instead of throwing them away!

These are just some of Ms Butler's crazy ideas. While we all agree that the environment is an important issue, shouldn't the ecology society be putting forward more practical ideas than this?

3 Look at the incorrect information in the article and decide what Tanya really said. You may need to listen to the talk again to do this.

4 What type of language do you think she used in her letter?

5 Write a plan of Tanya's letter.

6 Compare plans with your partner.

7 Write the letter from the plan. Remember to use reported speech when necessary.

GRAMMAR GR p186

It's time

1 Look at these sentences from the listening text:

It's high time a range of vegetarian dishes was on offer
It's time we had a balance of meat and vegetarian dishes

1 What time is referred to?
2 Which grammatical form is used?

2 Compare these two sentences. What is the difference in meaning?

It's (high) time we went.
It's time to go.

3 Finish each of the following sentences in such a way that it means exactly the same as the sentence printed before it.

1 This room hasn't been cleaned for ages.
It's time ____________________
2 The college has not been redecorated for years. It really needs doing.
It's time ____________________
3 I haven't eaten all day. I'm very hungry.
It's time ____________________
4 It's late, I should have left an hour ago.
It's time ____________________
5 My car's filthy, I really have it cleaned.
It's time ____________________

SPEAKING

Discuss some of the following ideas with your partner:

1 Animal liberationists are crazy extremists.
2 It's time factory farming was banned.
3 We should close zoos and return the animals to their natural environment.
4 The world would be a better place if everyone was a vegetarian.
5 It's time to give up the stresses of modern life and go back to growing our own food.
6 If we don't do more to protect the environment, many species will soon be as dead as the dinosaurs.

REVISION TEST 11

1 For each question 1 – 8 choose the word or phrase that best completes the sentence.

1 The book is ________ to be over 100 years old.
A told **B** believed **C** realised **D** seemed

2 As ________ as I receive the letter, I'll phone you.
A once **B** so **C** soon **D** far

3 Give me a ring when the concert ________.
A will end **B** ended **C** had ended **D** ends

4 I would like to apologise for ________ your birthday.
A forgetting **B** to forget **C** have forgotten **D** forget

5 He looks very much ________ his sister.
A same **B** as **C** like **D** so

6 As his granny lived alone, she bought a dog to keep her ________.
A up **B** friendly **C** together **D** company

7 I wish you ________ make so much noise when you come in late at night.
A hadn't **B** wouldn't **C** weren't **D** shouldn't

8 I came to this language school on the ________ of a friend.
A recommendation **B** proposal **C** indication **D** satisfaction

2 You will hear part of a radio programme about dinosaurs. For each of the questions 1–4 tick (✓) one of the boxes to show the correct answer.

1 The extinction of the dinosaurs
A took millions of years.
B was caused by disease.
C happened very quickly.
D followed a volcanic eruption.

A	
B	
C	
D	

2 Where is iridium found?
A Only in rocks from outer space.
B In areas near to volcanos.
C In rocks about 65 million years old.
D In rocks formed under water.

A	
B	
C	
D	

3 Why did the animals die?
A They were covered in dust.
B There were a number of meteorites.
C There was nothing to eat.
D They could not see the sun.

A	
B	
C	
D	

4 Why is the crater difficult to find?
A There may be more than one.
B It has been destroyed by the sea.
C It has been filled in.
D It is buried under more recent rock.

A	
B	
C	
D	

3 Fill each of the numbered blanks in the following passage. Use only one word in each space.

About 66 million years ________ (1), seventy percent of all living creatures including the dinosaurs are ________ (2) to have disappeared ________ (3) the surface of the Earth.

Scientists believe that this may ________ (4) been caused by a natural disaster on a ________ (5) large scale. One possible explanation is ________ (6) the earth was ________ (7) by an enormous asteroid about six miles ________ (8) diameter as it travelled through space.

Side effects of this disaster could have been the destruction of ________ (9) ozone layer, acid rain, global warming and the pollution of the atmosphere ________ (10) dust which blocked ________ (11) the sun.

Either one or a combination of ________ (12) effects could have ________ (13) the disappearance of the various species.

Scientists are ________ (14) searching for the site of the crater ________ (15) the asteroid must have ________ (16). This may be buried ________ (17) more recent rocks, or be lost somewhere on the seabed. Wherever ________ (18) is, it seems probable that the dinosaurs died out ________ (19) a result of an environmental disaster lasting only a ________ (20) years.

4 Complete the following sentences with a suitable expression formed from GET.

Example: I didn't really want to come, but I couldn't get *out of* it.

1 He is just getting ________ a bad attack of flu.
2 I tried to phone him a number of times but I couldn't get ________.
3 Susan wasn't sure about changing school, but she seems to be getting ________ very well at the new one.
4 When taking notes, it's impossible to get ________ every word the teacher says.
5 He's a very good teacher, he can get his message ________ to the students very clearly.
6 John wanted to suggest a new idea, but nobody really understood what he was getting ________.
7 Rachel doesn't have much money but she gets ________ somehow.
8 Do try to get your homework ________ on time this week.
9 That's not a serious problem, I'm sure we can get ________ it.
10 Serena asked the chemist for something to get ________ ________ her headache.

5 Choose one of the following compositions. Your answer must be of between 120 and 180 words.

1 You are asked to give a talk to a group of school children on the importance of recycling. What advice do you give them?

2 Describe what could be done to prevent the destruction of the rainforests.

6 In the following conversation the parts numbered 1-6 have been left out. Complete them suitably.

(Fred has recently moved to a new house and he is talking to his neighbour.)

Fred: Hello Mike. Can I ask you about the rubbish system here?

Mike: Of course. Go ahead.

Fred: What (1)____?

Mike: You have to leave it outside the front door in a plastic sack.

Fred: Where (2) ____?

Mike: The local council provides them every few months.

Fred: Is (3) ____?

Mike: No, it's collected twice a week, on Mondays and Thursdays.

Fred: Do (4) ____?

Mike: Yes, they do, very early. So it's best to put it out the night before.

Fred: Can (5) ____?

Mike: No, not everything. You mustn't put glass in the rubbish, of course.

Fred: What (6) ____?

Mike: There's a bottle bank at the end of the road. Near the supermarket.

Fred: OK. Thanks for the information.

UNIT 12 FINAL TOUCHES

SPEAKING

1 Look at photograph number 1 and discuss these questions with your partner.

1. Who are these people?
2. What are they doing? Why?
3. Where are they?
4. How do they each feel?

2 Listen to someone talking about the photograph.

1. Do you agree with what she says about the photo?
2. How much specialist vocabulary about boats do you hear?
3. How certain is the speaker about what she says? What language tells you this?

①

②

3 Look at photograph number 2. Use your imagination and the language in the box to talk about the people in this way:

1 Where are the people?
2 How do they feel?
3 What are they looking at?
4 What are they thinking?

It looks as if they...	I get the impression that he is...
They look + adjective	Maybe they're...
It looks like + (a) noun	Perhaps they're...
She seems to be + adjective	They might be
She seems to be + verb+ing	They could be
He appears to be + adjective	They may be
He appears to be + verb+ing	They must/can't be

4 Read this passage. Which of the two photos do you think it matches?

There was more than a little tension in the air, after all this was a new experience for all of us. The waiting had caused Maria to get a little bored, but the rest of us could sense that something really important was about to happen.

Listen to someone talking about the passage and linking it to a photo. Do you agree with the ideas expressed?

5 Read these two passages. Discuss with your partner which passage is describing photograph 1 on page 160.

1 **We left London around ten in the morning. The wind was getting up, but otherwise it was a fine day. Lois felt a bit apprehensive about the trip, but I was soon getting some practical advice from our two trainers on how to avoid running into the other traffic on the river.**

2 **It was quite a relief to be leaving London behind us. The weather was a bit better now and I no longer felt quite so seasick. As it was about an hour's trip to Southend, I left Jack talking to some other passengers and went down to the bar to get a drink.**

GRAMMAR *GR p186*

Question tags

1 Look at these sentences from the listening texts:

They must be going down towards the sea, ***mustn't they****?*
You can see the wind in their hair, ***can't you****?*
She looks pretty bored, ***doesn't she****?*

These are statements with question tags. With your partner discuss the following:

1 What are the rules for forming question tags?
2 When are question tags used?
3 How do we know if we should answer a question tag or not?

2 Add a question tag to each of these statements.

1 You're Joe's sister, ________ ?
2 It's a lovely day, ________ ?
3 She's finished her course, ________ ?
4 You went to that party, ________ ?
5 He always drives to work, ________ ?
6 You can give her a lift, ________ ?
7 You won't forget to ring Lesley, ________ ?
8 Let's play Scrabble, ________ ?
9 You've met Mr Simpson, ________ ?
10 You don't like tennis, ________ ?
11 You haven't done your homework, ________ ?
12 You'll have time for a cup of tea, ________ ?

FINAL TEST

Paper 1 Reading Comprehension (1 hour)

SECTION A

In this section you must choose the word or phrase which best completes each sentence. Indicate the letter A, B, C or D against the number of each item 1 to 25 for the word or phrase you choose.

1 I remember _______ the letter a few days before going on holiday.
A to receive **B** receiving **C** received **D** to have received

2 There was no _______ in continuing; for him the race was over.
A value **B** worth **C** point **D** profit

3 She had to pass all her exams or _______ she would have no holiday.
A instead **B** else **C** therefore **D** though

4 The headteacher again brought _______ the issue of reintroducing school uniforms.
A back **B** down **C** up **D** in

5 _______ the time you reach the station, the train will have left.
A At **B** On **C** By **D** In

6 I object _______ the proposal to restrict the use of cars in the city.
A at **B** with **C** for **D** to

7 Patrick must get out of the _______ of arriving late for meetings.
A habit **B** custom **C** use **D** fashion

8 The dinner party went on much longer than John had _______.
A expected **B** wondered **C** attended **D** appeared

9 _______ hard she worked, Louise never managed to finish her homework on time.
A Moreover **B** However **C** Although **D** Despite

10 She returned home to find her house had been _______ .
A broken **B** stolen **C** burgled **D** thieved

11 It was a _______ day, so I took my umbrella.
A rainfall **B** raining **C** rainy **D** rainstorm

12 If I were you, I _______ visit them without an invitation.
A won't **B** hadn't **C** don't **D** wouldn't

13 He was unable to ________ his graduation ceremony as he was abroad at the time.
A take part **B** respect **C** undertake **D** attend

14 ________ from a two-hour delay on the return flight, the holiday was very successful.
A Apart **B** Besides **C** Except **D** Although

15 When Rosemary is concentrating she ________ me of her grandmother.
A reminds **B** remembers **C** recalls **D** revises

16 It's high time we ________ cutting down the rainforests.
A stop **B** shall stop **C** have stopped **D** stopped

17 I'm thinking of ________ my house repainted.
A making **B** taking **C** doing **D** having

18 Having decided to buy a new greenhouse, he wrote ________ for some manufacturers' catalogues.
A off **B** up **C** down **D** out

19 Freshly ________ coffee usually tastes and smells better than instant coffee.
A crushed **B** reduced **C** smashed **D** ground

20 I would ________ you didn't smoke in the lounge, please.
A rather **B** like **C** ask **D** better

21 They ________ to meet outside the theatre at 7.45 pm.
A appointed **B** arranged **C** engaged **D** settled

22 When they built the new motorway they knocked ________ many old buildings along the route.
A over **B** down **C** out **D** away

23 'You can't play with your new toys ________ you finish up all your dinner' said Tessa's father.
A as long as **B** whether **C** if only **D** unless

24 The ________ of the first daffodils in spring reminded him of Samantha.
A view **B** scene **C** sight **D** watch

25 The doctor's house ________ at the junction of two busy roads.
A stands **B** rests **C** stays **D** seats

SECTION B

In this section you will find after each of the passages a number of questions or unfinished statements about the passage, each with four suggested answers or ways of finishing. You must choose the one which you think fits best according to the passage. Give one answer only to each question. Read each passage right through before choosing your answers.

FIRST PASSAGE

Although no note awaited her on the doorstep, no letter came and there were no phone calls, Anna knew the cat woman would come back on the following evening. Richard had advised her to go to the police if any threats were made. There would be no need to tell them she had been driving very fast. Anna thought the whole idea of going to the police bizarre. She rang up her friend Kate and told her all about it and Kate agreed that telling the police would be going too far.

The battered red car arrived at 7pm. Maria Jakob was dressed as she had been for her previous visit, but because it was rather cold, wore a jacket made of synthetic fur as well. From its harsh too-shiny texture there was no doubt it was synthetic but from a distance it looked like a black cat's pelt.

She had brought an album of photographs of her cats for Anna to see. Anna looked throught it — what else could she do? Some were recognisably of those she had seen through the windows. Those that were not, she supposed might be of animals now at rest under the wooden crosses in Maria Jakob's back garden. While she was looking at the pictures, Griselda, Anna's mother's cat, came in and jumped on to the cat woman's lap. 'They're very nice, very interesting,' Anna said. 'I can see you're devoted to your cats.'

'They're my life.'

A little humouring might be in order. 'When is the funeral to be?'

'I thought on Friday. Two o'clock on Friday. My sister will be there with her two. Cats don't usually take to car travel, that's why I don't often take any of mine with me, and shutting them up in cages goes against the grain, but my sister's two Burmese love the car, they'll go and sit in the car when it's parked. My friend from the Animal Rescue will come if she can get away and I've asked our vet but I don't hold out much hope there. He has his goat clinic on Fridays. I hope you'll come along.'

'I'm afraid I'll be at work.'

'It's no flowers by request. Donations to the Cats' Protection League instead. Any sum, no matter how small, gratefully received. Which brings me to money. You've got a cheque for me.'

'No I haven't, Mrs Yackle.'

'Miss. And it's Jakob. J.,A.,K.,O.,B. You've got a cheque for me for £799.

'I am not giving you any money, Miss Jakob. I'm very very sorry about your cat, about Melusina, I know how fond you were of her, but giving you compensation is out of the question. I'm sorry.'

The tears had come once more into Maria Jakob's eyes, had spilled over. Her face contorted with misery. It was the mention of the wretched thing's name, Anna thought. That was the trigger that started the weeping. A tear splashed on to one of the coarse red hands. Griselda opened her eyes and licked up the tear.

Maria Jakob pushed her other hand across her eyes. She blinked. 'We'll have to think of something else then,' she said.

'I beg your pardon?' Anna wondered if she had really heard right. Things couldn't be solved so simply.

'We shall have to think of something else. A way for you to make up to me for murder.'

'Look, I will give a donation to the Cats' Protection League. I'm quite prepared to give them — say £20.' Richard would be furious but perhaps she would not tell Richard. 'I'll give it to you, shall I, and then you can pass it on to them?'

'I certainly hope you will. Especially if you can't come to the funeral.'

That was the end of it then. Anna felt a great sense of relief. It was only now that she realised quite how it had got to her. It had actually kept her from sleeping properly. She phoned Kate and told her about the funeral and the goat clinic and Kate laughed and said, poor old thing. Anna slept so well that night that she did not notice the arrival of Griselda who, when she woke, was asleep on the pillow next to her face, but out of touching distance.

26 Why had Anna not phoned the police?
- A Because she had been driving fast.
- B She wasn't sure if the woman would come back.
- C She hadn't been threatened in any way.
- D It seemed an unnecessary thing to do.

27 Why did Anna look through the photographs?
- A She recognised some of the cats.
- B She was very interested in them.
- C She didn't know how to behave.
- D Maria made her look at them.

28 What invitation did Anna refuse?
- A To attend a goat clinic.
- B To visit the Animal Rescue.
- C To go to a funeral.
- D To meet Maria's sister.

29 Why does Maria ask Anna for £799?
- A As a donation to the Cats' Protection League.
- B Because Anna can't attend the funeral.
- C Because Anna has killed one of Maria's cats.
- D Because Maria's car has been damaged.

30 What is Kate's reaction to the story?
- A She doesn't take it seriously.
- B She is relieved that it is over.
- C She feels sorry for Anna.
- D She finds it frightening.

SECOND PASSAGE

The importance of temperature – How food poisoning is caused

Most food poisoning in this country is caused by five groups of bacteria — Campylobacter, Salmonella, Clostridium, Listeria and Staphylococcus. Even small numbers of Salmonella cells can cause food poisoning but other types of bacteria have to be present in large numbers before they make food dangerous. In other words, they have been allowed to grow and multiply for a sufficiently long time to produce large numbers of cells.

If Salmonella and Listeria are to cause problems, living cells of the bacteria have to be present in the food when it is eaten. Normal, but thorough, cooking should destroy these cells and render them harmless.

Staphylococci are different inasmuch as they produce toxin (a poisonous chemical) when they are actively growing. Even though cooking may destroy the bacterial cells, it is unlikely to inactivate the toxin.

Food producers do their best to make sure that food is not contaminated with any food-poisoning organisms. But if some should be in food, the maintenance of a cold temperature can do a lot to minimise growth and therefore the risk of food poisoning. The Food Hygiene (Amendment) Regulations 1990 requires that, from 1 April 1993, most short-life food must be kept at 5°C or colder after manufacture and throughout distribution and display. Keeping such a cold temperature will require many food companies to buy better refrigeration equipment so, until April 1993, a temperature of no warmer than 8°C must be maintained for those foods.

Although there is no law governing the performance of household refrigerators, you should use a thermometer to make sure your refrigerator is operating at 5°C or colder. Suitable thermometers are available in Sainsbury's stores which sell freezer accessories.

Once food has cooled to 5°C or colder, if any food poisoning bacteria are present most will grow only very slowly and it would take a long time for them to reach large enough numbers to cause a problem. But, if Listeria should be present, it will grow and multiply, even at refrigerator temperatures. And if the food is at 10°C, Listeria will grow more rapidly than any other organism.

Frozen foods are stored at -18°C throughout distribution and there is no possibility of bacterial cells growing and multiplying at that temperature.

But remember that neither chilling nor freezing kills all bacteria so it is very important to keep chilled foods chilled and frozen foods frozen until they are used. Once they reach room temperature, bacteria become active again and food deterioration starts or resumes from where it left off.

31 How is Salmonella different from other bacteria?

A It multiplies more quickly.
B A small amount can poison you.
C Only living cells cause poisoning.
D It causes other bacteria to grow.

32 How is Staphylococcus different from other bacteria?

A The cells are destroyed by thorough cooking.
B The cells take a long time to grow and multiply.
C The poison is not destroyed by cooking.
D A large number of cells are needed to poison you.

33 How does refrigeration help to reduce the risk of food poisoning?
- A It kills any bacteria that are in the food.
- B It stops the bacteria growing any more.
- C It prevents new bacteria entering the food.
- D It makes the bacteria grow more slowly.

34 How will the law change in 1993?
- A All chilled food will be displayed in refrigerators.
- B Shops will have to use new refrigeration equipment.
- C Once made, chilled food will have to be kept colder.
- D All refrigerators will have thermometers fitted.

35 What is it important to remember about chilled and frozen foods?
- A They are clear of bacteria and poisons whilst kept cold.
- B They should be used once they have reached room temperature.
- C Chilled foods should not be frozen completely.
- D They all contain Listeria which continues to grow in any case.

THIRD PASSAGE

'Parachuting changed my life!'

When Su Woods stepped out on to the tarmac of Thruxton airfield one sunny afternoon in 1974 to make her first parachute jump, she was not only about to make her childhood dream come true, she was also leaving her old life for a new one. Achieving her ambition was to transform her life. Eight years later, Su and her husband Dennis own the parachute club where Su made her first jump, and where they met.

'Parachuting has changed my life enormously,' Su says.'When I think back to the first day I came, watching all the experienced jumpers and free-fallers and feeling so nervous, I have to keep telling myself that the club's all ours. I've made 100 jumps now — that's quite a lot. But there are plenty of members here who are much more advanced than I am.

'It's so exhilarating you don't get frightened. Everything to do with parachuting in this country is so highly regulated. You can't just go up in a plane and jump out of it. You must have proper training. Safety precautions are rigorously enforced. At first, you have a static line attached to your parachute linking it to the aeroplane. As you fall free, the line pulls the parachute open. It's not until you've reached a certain standard that you're allowed to open your own parachute, so there's not really any danger. A feeling of fear at the thought of jumping out of a plane at 2,500 ft is only natural sometimes!

'When you're first told you're ready to go up, you get really nervous. You step out on to the platform, the instructor says "Go", and then you're in the air. It's so exhilarating, you can't imagine what you were afraid of. Even now, I get nervous when I go up for a jump. But as soon as you're coming down, peace all around you, the earth below, it's wonderful.'

Juggling her career as editor of an internal newspaper for a major British company with sorting out a new house, managing the parachute club and pursuing her favourite hobby, means that things like housework and washing up can get badly neglected. 'But then,' Su says, 'it's a question of priorities. I'd rather parachute than spend Saturdays cleaning the house.

'We try to travel the 40 miles from home to the club as often as we can and, of course, we're there all weekend. That's the best time. It's a very sociable place — families come to watch and take part, and we have a lot of charity jumps, which is nice.'

36 What reasons did Su have for beginning parachuting?
A It was something she had always wanted to do.
B She had wanted to change her life completely.
C She wanted to show her children what she could do.
D She had married the owner of the club.

37 What happens when you start jumping?
A You jump with the parachute already open.
B You always jump with another person.
C You are not allowed to open your own parachute.
D You remain connected to the ground.

38 What does Su say about the emotions involved in parachuting?
A You never get over the fear of falling.
B You get very nervous before jumping out.
C You are only nervous the first few times you jump.
D You are more nervous with the instructor.

39 How has parachuting changed Su's life?
A She has given up her job.
B She now jumps for a living.
C She now owns the parachute club.
D She goes parachuting every day.

40 How does Su spend most of her weekend?
A Looking after her family.
B Doing work for charity.
C Following her favourite hobby.
D Enjoying social life at the club.

Paper 2 Composition (1½ hours)

Write two only of the following composition exercises. Your answers must follow exactly the instructions given and must be of between 120 and 180 words each.

1 You have been asked to give a talk to a group of young people about the importance of a good balanced diet. What advice do you give them?

2 Some people think it is wrong to use animals to test new cosmetics and drugs. Do you agree?

3 You have recently taken up a new sport or pastime. Write a letter to a friend describing the activity and saying why it would be a good thing for him or her to take it up as well.

4 'Oh no, not again!' Write a story which begins OR ends with these words.

5 Based on your reading of one of the set texts, describe the importance of one of the main characters to the story.

Paper 3 Use Of English (2 hours)

1 *Fill each of the numbered blanks in the following passage. Use only one word in each space.*

In 1856, James Lofthouse, a chemist ________ (1) the fishing port of Fleetwood produced ________ (2) first Fisherman's Friend. The local sailors often suffered ________ (3) coughs and so Lofthouse produced a lozenge that relieved the symptoms.

The Lofthouse family continued to produce the sweets and sell ________ (4) in their shop ________ (5) over a century. Then in 1963, Doreen Cowell, a young local woman, was employed ________ (6) a shop assistant. Doreen noticed ________ (7) popular the lozenges were and how ________ (8) of Fleetwood's summer visitors bought them and then wrote to the shop asking ________ (9) more supplies.

Doreen decided to market the sweets ________ (10) widely and went to visit the areas ________ (11) which she ________ (12) received most letters, to encourage the local shops to ________ (13) them. The popularity of the lozenges soon spread and ________ (14) 1971 a new factory had been ________ (15) in Fleetwood to produce them. By this time Doreen ________ (16) married into the Lofthouse family and become Managing Director of the company.

The first export market was Norway, ________ (17) Fisherman's Friend soon proved to be as popular in hot countries ________ (18) in cold countries. Today, 250 tons of lozenges are produced in Fleetwood every month, and the familiar packets are printed ________ (19) twenty-one different languages for export all ________ (20) the world.

2 *Finish each of the following sentences in such a way that it means exactly the same as the sentence printed before it.*

Example: I haven't laughed so much for ages.

It's ages *since I laughed so much.*

1 Victor started collecting postage stamps twenty-five years ago.

Victor has ____

2 Whose wallet is this?

Who does ____

3 The translation course takes two years.

It's a ____

4 Daphne writes more clearly than Caterina.

Caterina doesn't ____

5 Although she had an injured ankle, Esther still won the tennis match.

Despite ______________________________

6 It's not my fault if the television doesn't work.

Don't ______________________________

7 'Can I have a new pair of football boots?' Robert asked his father.

Robert asked ______________________________

8 Chris failed his driving test because he didn't have enough lessons.

If Chris ______________________________

9 It was such a long journey that they were all asleep by the time they arrived.

The journey ______________________________

10 Louisa has taught her children how to prepare their own meals.

Louisa's children ______________________________

3 *Complete the following sentences with one word formed from the word* LATE.

Example: He's not here at the moment, can you phone back *later?*

1 He was given the sack because of repeated _______.

2 Although he was ill earlier in the year, he's been looking much better _______ .

3 She rushed out to buy the _______ disc by her favourite group.

4 The performance starts at 8pm sharp and _______ will not be admitted.

5 She missed her bus and had to catch a _______ one.

4 *Below are five groups of three words. In the spaces write the one word which describes each group.*

Example: bookcase, wardrobe, sofa, *furniture*

1 lounge, study, kitchen ______________

2 knife, fork, spoon ______________

3 oil, coal, gas ______________

4 theft, burglary, shoplifting ______________

5 chess, backgammon, hangman ______________

5 *Make all the changes and additions necessary to produce, from the following sets of words and phrases, sentences which together make a complete letter. Note carefully from the example what kind of alterations need to be made. Write each sentence in the space provided.*

Example: I be very surprised/receive/letter/you this morning.

I was very surprised to receive a letter from you this morning.

43 Upton Road
Snowfield
Milton
MT3 8PT

12th March

The Manager
Graziella's
5 High Street
Milton
MT1 3QP

Dear Sir or Madam

I write/reply/your advertisement/this week's Milton Evening News.

1 ______________________________

You say/you look/sales assistant/who be able/speak Italian/English.

2 ______________________________

I just finish/one-year translation course/at local Polytechnic.

3 ______________________________

At/end/course/pass all/exams/ good marks.

4 ______________________________

Before I start it/I spend/year/Italy/working/clothes shop.

5 ______________________________

Although I be born/England/I spend a lot of time/Italy/as my mother be Italian.

6 ______________________________

I be very grateful/you send me further details about/job/application form.

7 ______________________________

I look forward/hear/you.

8 ______________________________

Yours faithfully,

Erica McDonald

6 *All students who attend the Fieldside Summer Schools have the opportunity to take part in extra afternoon activities. Below you will find some information about the activities and details of three of the students, Simon, Jenny and Barbara. Decide which activities they are likely to choose and give your reasons. Write your answers in the spaces provided. You do not need to use all the information.*

COURSES

EasyDrive EasyDrive allows you to begin driving lessons while you are still only sixteen years old. The lessons are on private land, safe from other traffic. First you learn basic driving skills, then in the more advanced course we take you round a specially prepared route with traffic lights and road signs.	*Horse Riding* Learn to ride a horse safely and confidently. Our First Lessons package includes all the basic training necessary to control a horse. The lessons take place inside our specially built riding school. We provide experienced trainers and, of course, a beautiful horse! Please bring your own riding hat.
Parascending This is the experience of a lifetime! You have all the excitement of parachuting, without any last-minute panic about jumping out of a plane. You will be lifted from the ground to a height of 150 metres and fly above beautiful countryside for about ten minutes. You can even take your camera! The price includes full training and equipment.	*Computer Skills* This course in DTP (Desk Top Publishing) shows you how to design and print your own high quality professional-looking magazines and newspapers using just a simple home computer. You don't have to be a computer genius to enjoy the course, although it helps if you can already use a computer keyboard.

STUDENTS

Simon — aged 15, rather quiet person, likes machines, wants to be a scientist

Jenny — aged 18, loves cars and driving, goes on adventure holidays, doesn't play any sports but ready to try anything new

Barbara — aged 17, very keen photographer, likes walking and climbing, healthy and good at sports

I think Simon ______________________________

____

____

I suppose Jenny ______________________________

____

____

Barbara ______________________________

____

____

Paper 4 Listening Comprehension (about 30 minutes)

You will hear part of a radio interview with a plastic surgeon. For questions 1 to 5 tick (✓) one of the boxes A, B, C or D to show the correct answer.

FIRST PART

1 What type of work is most common in plastic surgery?

A Helping people who have been involved in accidents.
B Repairing the work of unqualified surgeons.
C Helping people who are embarrassed about their looks.
D Improving or preserving the looks of famous people.

A	
B	
C	
D	

2 What does Mr Johnstone say to people who want plastic surgery but look alright?

A He explains why it is not necessary.
B He encourages them to have the operation.
C He sends them to another surgeon.
D He refers them to their own doctor.

A	
B	
C	
D	

3 In which situation is plastic surgery not available?

A For people who are shy.
B For people who are overweight.
C Where there are risks of failure.
D For people who cannot pay.

A	
B	
C	
D	

4 Why do some people answer advertisements in magazines?

A They do not want to talk to their own doctor.
B They do not want to talk about their medical history.
C They do not realise that their doctor can help.
D They do not believe they have a medical problem.

A	
B	
C	
D	

5 What is Mr Johnstone's opinion of surgeons who advertise?

A They may be dishonest.
B They may not be surgeons.
C They may not know the patient.
D They may be more expensive.

A	
B	
C	
D	

SECOND PART

You will hear an interview about Electronic Organisers. For questions 6 to 11 listen and tick one of the boxes A, B, C or D to show the correct answer.

6 How is the Electronic Organiser like a computer?

A It is the same size.
B It has a large screen.
C It works in the same way.
D It will print out pages.

A	
B	
C	
D	

7 Why are Electronic Organisers used in some shops?
A They are simple to operate.
B The shop assistants like them.
C They are easy to carry.
D They replace a normal computer.

A	
B	
C	
D	

8 The Blunt Electronic Organiser is
A the same size as a diary.
B the same shape as a wallet.
C the same price as a computer.
D the same weight as a calculator.

A	
B	
C	
D	

9 The Electronic Organiser can find a phone number using only
A the name.
B the address.
C the town.
D the postcode.

A	
B	
C	
D	

10 What is Eric Newman's advice about Electronic Organisers?
A Buy a computer instead.
B Wait before buying anything.
C Throw them away.
D Give them as presents.

A	
B	
C	
D	

11 How does the interviewer feel about Electronic Organisers?
A Enthusiastic.
B Worried.
C Fascinated.
D Doubtful.

A	
B	
C	
D	

THIRD PART

For each of the questions 12 - 18 tick (✓) the box to show whether the statements are true or false.

	True	False
12 The restaurants all have the same furniture.		
13 The director's house is decorated in the same way as the restaurant.		
14 Each restaurant serves some local specialities.		
15 If the pictures were different prices would be higher.		
16 Restaurant managers are not allowed to vary the standard of service.		
17 The director thinks it would be bad to offer a special service.		
18 The interviewer likes the restaurants as they are.		

Paper 5 Interview

The theme of this interview is **work**.

①

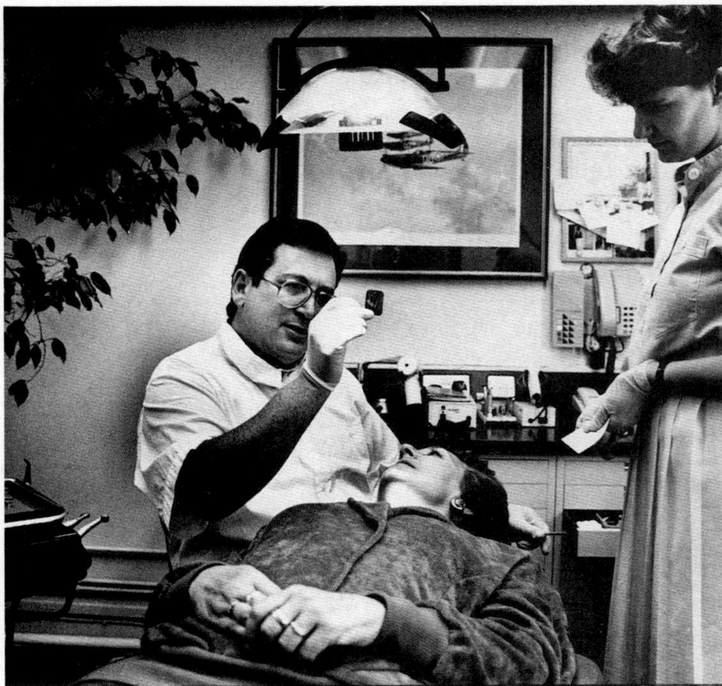

②

③

1 Look at one or more of the photographs.

2 Describe/compare - the jobs shown.
- how the people feel about their jobs.

3 Discuss - the importance of job satisfaction.
- the relative merits of working with
- people, computers, money, your hands,etc.

4 Read one or more of the following passages. Match one or more of the passages with the photographs, giving your reasons.

A My work is very satisfying. It takes several days of hard work to change a piece of wood into something which you can begin to recognise as a musical instrument. I hope that the sound which is produced will give pleasure to many people.

B The people who come here are often nervous and, of course, sometimes in pain and really very upset. I try to make them as comfortable as possible. A sense of humour is essential for this job. Although at the end of a long day it's difficult to smile and look happy!

C Business was quiet yesterday on the London Exchange. Dealers said that the rise in the Japanese Yen and fears of another increase in German interest rates had little effect, and investors were waiting for the US trade figures which will be announced next week.

5 Look at the list of jobs in the box ,and discuss:

Either:

How stressful are each of the following jobs?
Say what creates stress for the people doing each of these jobs and whether this is balanced by good things about the job.

Or:

Choose the five most and the five least stressful from this list of jobs, saying why you think each job is stressful or not.

stockbroker	marketing manager	fire officer
nurse	gardener	telephonist
teacher	hairdresser	pilot
lawyer	waiter	secretary
train driver	bank cashier	police officer

GRAMMAR REFERENCE

UNIT 1

Present Simple (page 2)

This tense is used to describe habits, states and routines - that is, things which usually or always happen or which are usually or always true. In many languages, this tense is also used to describe what is happening now. Notice that this is not the case in English.

Uses:

a To talk about things which are always true:
*Water **boils** at 100° centigrade.*
*He **has** blue eyes.*

b To talk about habits and routines:
*I **walk** to school* (usually).

Present Continuous

This tense is used to describe what is happening now:
*He **is studying** French.*

NB when describing a photograph or picture, we usually use the Present Continuous – we talk about it as if it were happening now:
*The man in the picture **is crossing** the road.*

Order of Adjectives (page 3)

The following order is often used, but there are many exceptions.

Opinion	size	shape	colour	material	+ noun
horrible	small	square	blue	nylon	headscarf
wonderful	big	round	yellow	cotton	teddy bear

NB It is unusual to use more than two or three adjectives before a noun.

In Case (page 8)

In case is used when we want to be prepared for something that may happen. **In case** is followed by the Present Simple tense but refers to future or present time.

In case can also be used with the Past tense:
*I took an overcoat **in case it was cold**.*

In case + should can be used for things which are very unlikely or in more formal situations in the present and future.
*You are advised to wear a seatbelt **in case there should** be an accident.*

UNIT 2

To be used to + ing/noun (page 19)

This form is used to indicate how a person feels about something or about doing something. It expresses how comfortable or familiar a thing or action is to them.
*Pablo **is used to eating** later in the evening.*
*I am **used to the cold**.*

To get used to

shows a change in how we feel about something:
*I **can't get used to** this weather* (I'm not able to change my feelings).
*I **am getting used to eating** later.* (My feelings about it are changing with experience).
*I've **got used to drinking** this strange water* (My feelings have now changed as a result of experience).

Present Perfect (page 21)

This tense is formed by: *Have* + past participle of the verb.
The present perfect is used

a to talk about past experiences in your life:
*I've **been to** Egypt three times.*

b to talk about things which have happened in unfinished periods of time:
*I've **drunk** too much coffee today.*
*I've **learnt** how to use a PC.*

c to talk about things which have recently happened:
*She**'s just written** a letter to him.*

Present Perfect vs Past Simple (page 22)

If you need to decide which tense to use, ask yourself the question When?
*I**'ve never been** to Italy, but I went to Greece last summer.*
*I**'ve never been** to Italy* – When? In my life (Present Perfect)
*I **went** to Greece last summer* – When? Last summer (Present Simple).

Comparison of Adjectives (page 28)

One-syllable adjectives	two-syllable adjectives	three or more syllable adjectives
calm-calmer	tidy-tidier	enthusiastic-more enthusiastic
old-older	dirty-dirtier	responsible-more responsible
hot-hotter	helpful-more helpful	
wet-wetter	handsome-more handsome	

Exceptions: good - better
bad - worse
far - further/farther (further, but not farther, can mean 'more' or 'in addition': *tell me if you need any **further** information*)

One-syllable adjectives and two-syllable adjectives ending in **y** form the comparison by adding **er**. Single consonants at the end of the word double before adding **er**.

Two-syllable adjectives ending in other letters and all adjectives of three or more syllables form the comparison by adding - 'more'.

Positive comparisons are made with than:	*John **is older than** Mary.*
Comparisons of equality are made with as:	*John **is as tall as** Mary*
the same + noun + as:	*Jim **is the same height as** Sue.*
Negative comparisons are made with not as:	*This baby **is not as young as** that one.*
Less is used where the adjective takes more in the positive:	*John **is less enthusiastic than** Mary.*

NB Not as .... as is possible with all adjectives. Less .... than is usually found in more formal language.

Superlatives

The superlative is formed by adding 'est' to one-syllable adjectives, 'iest' to two-syllable adjectives ending in 'y' and 'most' before longer adjectives:
*It's **the oldest building** in the city.*
*It was **the prettiest village** I had ever visited.*
*He is **the most enthusiastic student** in the class.*

Causative Have (page 35)

This form exists in a variety of tenses and in each case it is the verb 'to have' which indicates the tense. The verb indicating the action is always the past participle:
I'm having my car repaired (this means that someone is repairing my car).

Needs Doing (page 35)

This form is used to indicate that a certain job should be done, but we do not know, or do not want to know, who is going to do the job:
*The windows **need cleaning*** (They are dirty).
*The tape recorder **needs mending*** (it is broken).

UNIT 3

For/Since (page 39)

For and **since** are used with perfect tenses to indicate length of time.
Since can also be used with the Past Simple.

Since refers to a date in the past and is used to talk about things happening between then and now.
For refers to the period of time that has passed between a point of time in the past and now.

*I've known Mary **since March** – I've known Mary **for three months*** (it is now May).

Since can also be used in the middle of sentences which begin with a time period:
***It's a long time since** I've seen you* (I haven't seen you for a long time)

Since + Past Simple:
***It's two years since** I left the army* (I left the army two years ago - finished action in the past).

UNIT 4

Past Simple/Past Continuous (page 49).

The Past Simple is used

a to talk about events in the past:
*I **went** to the cinema **last night**.*

b to talk about events that happened one after another:
*I **finished** my homework and **sat down** to watch TV.*

The Past Continuous is used to talk about events which had begun but hadn't finished at a specific time in the past:
***I was watching TV at 9.00** yesterday evening.*

The Past Simple and Continuous are used together:

a when one action is interrupted by another:
I was watching TV when the lights went out.

b when one action takes place during a longer one:
***When I was shopping** in Oxford Street **I saw a car accident**.*

Deductions (page 51)

Modal verbs are used to say how sure or unsure we are about things:
*This **can't be** his mother, she's not old enough (I'm sure it isn't his mother).*
*He **could be** a teacher.*
*It **might be** her birthday today* (It's possible but I'm not sure).
*This **may be** Jane's pen.*

In the past, these verbs are formed with *have*:
*It **must have been** his house.*
*That **can't have been** his mother.*

Relative Clauses (page 55)

Relative Clauses can be 'defining' or 'non-defining'. They begin with a relative pronoun – *who* or *that* used for people, and *which* or *that* in other cases.

Defining relative clauses identify nouns – they tell us which person, thing etc, the speaker means:
*The girl **who sits** next to me is Japanese.*
(no punctuation surrounding this type of clause).

The relative pronoun can be omitted if it is the object of the clause:
*The girl **(that) I spoke to** was Japanese.*

Non-defining relative clauses give extra information about a person or thing:
*Mr Brown, **who is an electrician**, mended our kitchen light.*
(This extra information is enclosed by commas).

Whose is used to indicate possession:
*My brother, **whose house was burgled last week**, has been asked to help with police investigations.*
You can't use 'that' or omit the relative pronoun in non-defining relative clauses.

UNIT 5

Linking Words (page 63)

1 **After/After that**

After is generally followed by a noun, gerund or phrase:
***After coffee** we went home.*
***After drinking** our coffee we went home.*
***After we had drunk our coffee** we went home.*

When **after** is used we are saying that the events happened in the order in which they are mentioned.
After + first event + second event.

2 **After that/Afterwards**

refer to something already mentioned.

First event + **afterwards** + second event:
*We had coffee. **After that** we went home.*
***Afterwards** we went home.*

3 **Before**

Before follows the same rules as after when it is at the beginning of a sentence. It can be followed by a noun, gerund or phrase.
When **before** is used at the beginning of a sentence it indicates that the two events which are mentioned are in reverse order:
Before + second event + first event.
***Before** I paid the bill I checked the total to make sure it was correct.*

However, when **before** is used between two events the order is different:
First event + **before** + second event.
*I checked my change **before** I left the shop.*

4 **Although/Despite**

These are used to indicate contrast:
Although is followed by a subject and verb
***Although** there was very little snow, the skiing resort was crowded.*

Despite is followed by:
the fact that + subject + verb.
***Despite the cold weather**, we decided to climb the mountain.*
***Despite feeling** cold, we decided to climb the mountain.*

NB We can also say **even though (although)**
in spite of (despite).

Used To + Infinitive (page 66)

This tells us about things that happened in the past but which don't happen now. These are things which happened regularly over a long period of time.

*He **used to play football** when he was a child.*

Does he play football now? (no)
Did he play football often? (yes)

NB **Used to** does not exist in the present. The present of **used to** is **usually**.

Past Perfect (page 67)

When we tell a story, we set a time in the past in which the narrative takes place. When we refer to actions and periods before that, the Past Perfect is used:
*When we got back to the house, **he had removed** the furniture.*

UNIT 6

Time and Money expressions as adjectives (page 76)

*It's a **four-hour flight** from London to Athens*

ADJ + NOUN
(The flight from London to Athens takes four hours).

*He had to pay a **ten-pound parking fine***

ADJ + NOUN
(He had to pay a fine of ten pounds).

NB When the price or the time are used as an adjective they have no plural form.

Compound Adjectives (page 76)

These are formed when a noun and adjective, or verb and adjective, are combined with a hyphen to form an adjectival phrase.

A girl with blue eyes = A blue-eyed girl.
A woman who looks friendly = A friendly-looking woman.

To avoid sentences becoming lists of adjectives, it is good style to use compound adjectives before the main noun, especially when further adjectives follow:
***A tall grey-haired man** with green eyes and a moustache.*

Future Time (page 82)

1 The Present Simple is used when we talk about timetables and things which happen at fixed times and so cannot be changed:
*The flight **lands at 16.00**.*

The important question to ask yourself is: Can I change it - is it my decision?

2 The Present Continuous is used to talk about plans which we have already made with somebody else:
***I'm meeting** the manager at **2.30**.*

The important questions to ask yourself are: Have I already decided?
Have I made an arrangement with someone else?

3 Going to + infinitive is used for future plans and intentions that involve only ourselves, or where no definite arrangement has been made:
***I'm going to** learn Russian **next year**.*

Compare: *My Russian classes **start** next week* (it doesn't depend on me).
***I'm starting** Russian classes next week* (I've decided and I've arranged to join the class).

UNIT 7

-ing Form/Infinitive (page 89)

The commonest verbs which are followed by the -ing form are:

admit appreciate avoid consider delay deny detest dislike endure enjoy escape excuse face feel like finish forgive give up can't help imagine involve mention mind miss postpone practise put off resent resist risk can't stand suggest understand

The commonest verbs which are followed directly by an infinitive are:

afford agree appear arrange ask attempt bear begin care choose consent dare decide determine expect fail forget happen hate help hesitate hope intend learn like love manage mean neglect offer prefer prepare pretend promise propose refuse regret remember seem start trouble try want wish

Some of these verbs can also be followed by the -ing form, often with a different meaning.

Too/Enough (page 90)

Too and **enough** are opposite concepts used to talk about quantity and degree.

This house is too small = This house ***is not large enough***.

Too is used before adjectives (too hot); **Enough** is used after adjectives (cold enough).

Too is used before quantifiers and nouns: *Too many/few people* (countable noun).
Too much/little water (uncountable noun).

Enough is used directly with countable and uncountable nouns:
There ***are not enough*** *plates; There* ***is not enough*** *rice.*

Conditional 0/1 (page 92)

The zero conditional uses *if* or *when* to say what always or usually happens in a given situation:
When you ***press*** *this button, a bell* ***rings***.

The first conditional is used to predict what will happen given certain other facts. We use it for things that will probably happen in the real future and for predictions:
If I ***see*** *her,* ***I'll give*** *her the message.*
If it ***rains***, ***there'll be*** *a lot of traffic.*

Prefer/Rather (page 93)

a **I prefer** is used to refer to a general situation:
I ***prefer eating*** *Greek food to French food* (always/usually).

b **I'd prefer** is used to refer to a specific situation:
I'd prefer to go *to a restaurant* (now/on this occasion).

NB **I'd rather** + infinitive without 'to' can be used in place of **I'd prefer**.

Unless/If (page 94)

If refers to a positive condition: *If I* ***win I'll be*** *happy.*

Unless refers to a negative condition: *Unless I* ***win****/If I* ***don't win*** *I* ***won't be*** *happy.*

Future Time (Will + Infinitive) (page 96)

This form is used when we make decisions, offers and promises at the time of speaking:
What ***shall I*** *have? Let's see ..... Oh yes,* ***I'll have*** *a salad* (I'm deciding now).

A: *Have a lovely holiday!*
B: *Thanks.* ***I'll send*** *you a card.* (I promise).

A: *On no, I've left my bag in the car.*
B: ***I'll go*** *back and get it for you.* (I offer).

UNIT 8

The Passive (page 104)

The passive voice is formed by making the object of the active phrase into the subject of a new phrase:
Active – *I* ***wash*** *my car every week.*
Passive – *My car* ***is washed*** *every week.*

Passive voice equivalents exist for all major active tenses.

The passive is used in three main ways:

a To describe a process.

b When the action is more important than who does it:
The photocopier ***was repaired*** *in two hours.*

c When we do not know, or do not want to say, who does the action:
A window ***has been broken***.

NB The agent (by ....) is only used when it includes important information:
America ***was discovered*** *by Columbus in 1492.*

Never add 'by someone' to a passive phrase.

Will/Going to (Predictions) (page 109)

When making predictions we can use **will** or **going to**.

Will is used more to express the speaker's own opinion: *I think **it'll be** a good party.*

Going to is used when there is evidence of the future event:
*She**'s going to have** a baby.*

Conditional 2 (page 113)

Formed with If + past tense, subject + would.

This is used to predict what would happen given an improbable or hypothetical situation.
*If I **were** a fish, I **would live** in the sea* (but I'm not!).

Compare:

a *If it **rains**, I'**ll take** an umbrella.*
(I think it is probably going to rain - first conditional).
b *If I **went**, I **wouldn't speak** to him* (I am probably not going).

UNIT 9

So/Such (page 118)

So is used for countable and uncountable adjectives to make them stronger:
*This sport is **so** dangerous.*

And to link them to resulting actions:
*It was **so** cold that I wore two pairs of socks.*

Such can be used in a similar way with adjective and noun groups:
*It is **such** a dangerous sport* (Countable).
*It is **such** cold weather* (Uncountable).
*It was **such** cold weather that I wore two pairs of socks.*

So can be used with quantifiers:
*There was **so many/few** people that I could not breathe* (Countable).
*There was **so much/little** rice that we couldn't eat it all* (Uncountable).

Such can only be used with quantifiers that have an indefinite article:
*There were **such a lot** of people that...*
*There was **such a lack** of water that...*

Present Perfect Continuous (page 120)

The Present Perfect Continuous is used for activities

a which take place over an extended period of time, or which are repeated often in an extended period of time:
*I'**ve been playing** tennis for five years* (regularly).
*I'**ve been playing** tennis all morning* (continuously).

b which began in the past and either continue or have finished in the present time period specified:
*I'**ve been writing** letters today* (today has not finished).
*I'**ve been reading** in English this morning* (I have not had lunch yet).
NB I am not necessarily writing or reading now.

c which are general rather than specific or counted:
*I'**ve been listening** to a lot of classical music lately.*

Regrets (I Wish/If Only) (page 122)

Past regrets can be expressed by using **I wish/if only** + Past Perfect.

I went for a picnic. It rained.
(When? – in the past).
I feel sad. (Why? – because it spoilt the picnic) = ***I wish/If only** it **hadn't rained***.

In this phrase we are expressing the fact that we would like to change what happened but it is impossible and so we feel sad.

***I wish/If only** I **hadn't argued** with my father* (but I did and I can't change it now; I'm sorry about it – I regret it).

I regret is followed by + ing, and is normally used for events which are in our control. It is a more formal way of expressing our feelings than **I wish/if only**.

Conditional 3 (page 123)

This tense is formed with Past Perfect, would + have + Past Participle. It refers to past time – to things that cannot now be changed:
*If it **had rained**,* (did it rain? – No)
*I **would have taken** an umbrella* (did I take an umbrella? – No. Why? – because it didn't rain).

*If it **hadn't been** sunny,* (was it sunny? – Yes).
*I **wouldn't have got sunburnt*** (did I get sunburnt? – Yes).

Notice that in speech the third conditional is nearly always contracted:
*If **I'd seen** him, **I'd have said** hello.*

In writing we often contract *had* and *would* but not *have* in third conditional sentences.

UNIT 10

Modal Verbs – Obligation (page 133)

The meaning of the various verbs can be summarised as follows:

Positive:	*You must go/You have to go*	it's obligatory, you have no choice.
	You need to go/You should go	it's very advisable, but you choose.
	You ought to go	I advise you to go, but you choose.
	You can go	if you want, you choose.
	You may go	You have my permission to go.
Negative:	*You mustn't go/You can't go*	it's forbidden, you have no choice.
	You shouldn't go/You oughtn't to go	I advise you not to go, but you choose.
	You don't have to go	
	/You don't need to go	it's not obligatory, you choose.
	You needn't go	it's not necessary, you choose.

Make,Let,Allow (page 135).

Make + infinitive is used to express obligation.
*They **make** you **wear** a uniform at my school* (active).
*You **are made to wear** a uniform at my school* (passive).

Let + infinitive is used to express permission in the active:
*They **let** you park here on Saturdays.*

Allow + infinitive with to is used to express permission in the passive:
*You **are allowed** to park here on Saturdays.*

Wishes (page 140)

a **To wish** can be used as a simple verb: *I **wish** you a Merry Christmas.*

b **Wish** + Past Perfect is used to express past regrets (See page 183)

c **Wish** + was/were/had is used to express wishes about states:
*I **wish** I **had** blue eyes* (but I haven't).
*I **wish** he **was/were** rich* (but he isn't).

d **Wish** + could is used to express wishes about actions:
*I **wish** I **could** drive* (but I'm not able to).
*I **wish** you **could** dance* (but you are not able to).

e **Wish** + would is used to express annoyance at the habits of others:
*I **wish** you **wouldn't** sing in the bath* (I would like you to stop, but you won't).
*He **wishes** it **would** stop raining* (He'd like it to stop raining, but he can't change it).

UNIT 11

Reported Statements (page 148)

Most tenses in direct speech change in reported speech:

Present Simple	Past Simple
Present Perfect	Past Perfect
Present Perfect Continuous	Past Perfect Continuous
Present Continuous	Past Continuous
Past Simple	Past Perfect
Past Continuous	Past Perfect Continuous.

NB the Past Perfect remains the same in reported speech.

Other similar forms change in similar ways:

am going to	**was** going to
am used to doing	**was** used to doing
have to	**had** to
am able	**was** able
have something done	**had** something done.

There are occasions where you needn't change the tense:

a where facts are still true: *'My name **is** Paul'. – He said his name **is** Paul*

b Past Simple → Past Perfect depends on time references:
*'Peter **left** when I arrived' – she said Peter **left** when she arrived.* (Time references are clear - no need to change).
*'I **was** sick.' – She said she **had been** sick*
(Here the Past Simple (she was) could be misinterpreted as representing the Present Simple i.e. she is sick now).

Modal verbs can be divided into those that change and those that do not.

These can change:		These stay the same:
Can	*Could*	*Should*
May	*Might*	*Could*
Will	*Would*	*Would*
Must	*Had to*	*Ought*
Shall	*Should.*	*Might*

NB Would does not change to would have in reported speech.

Time Indicators (page 149)

Main changes:

today	that day
now	then
this	that
here	there
ago	before/previously
tomorrow	the next day/the following day
yesterday	the day before/the previous day
last night	the night before/the previous night
next week	the following week/the week after (that).

Reported Questions (page 151)

a WH questions: *'What time **is** it, Jenny?' – Nick asked Jenny what time it **was**.*
Do not forget to change the word order, because in reported speech these are not questions any more.

b Yes/No questions: *'**Are** you **coming** to the cinema, Jenny?' – Nick asked Jenny **whether/if** she **was** coming to the cinema.*

c Requests: *'**Would** you **pass** the salt please, Sid?'*
This type of question can be reported in full:
*Tom asked Sid **if** he **would pass** him the salt.*
or with an infinitive, which summarises the action:
*Tom asked Sid **to pass** him the salt.*

d Orders: usually an imperative:
*'**Go** to your room!' - Sarah's mother told her **to go** to her room.*

Impersonal Passive (page 154)

This form is used with certain verbs when we are not sure about the truth of the information:
He is said to be living in the USA (Some people say he is living in the USA, but it may not be true).

Other useful verbs are: *reported to be, believed to be, thought to be, understood to be.*

Reporting Verbs (page 155)

Often the meaning of a sentence in direct speech is summarised by a verb in reported speech.
'Would you like to go to the cinema, Jane?' ***said*** *Eric. – Eric* ***invited*** *Jane to the cinema.*

Other useful verbs of this type are found on page 00.

There are 3 main types:

Type A: Verb + person + infinitive with 'to'.
He ***told me to sit*** *down.*

Type B: Verb + infinitive with 'to'.
She ***agreed to give*** *him a reference.*

Type C: Verb + 'ing'.
She ***regretted leaving*** *her job.*

NB *He* ***apologised for losing*** *the report.*

It's (high) time + subjunctive (page 156).

This form is used when something needs doing urgently:
It's (high) time we went (subjunctive). (Adding 'high' makes this form stronger.)

This means we should have already gone – it is stronger than *It's time to go*.
NB The subjunctive is formed in the same way as the past tense.

UNIT 12

Looks/Seems/Appears (page 160)

These phrases are useful for describing photographs:

It looks as if they + verb.
They look + adjective.
It looks like + (a) noun.

She seems to be + adjective.
She seems to be + verb + ing.
He appears to be + adjective.
He appears to be + verb + ing.

I get the impression that he is ...
Maybe they're...
Perhaps they're...

See also **Deductions** (page 51).

Question Tags (page 161)

A question tag is a short interrogative phrase to a statement.
It's cold (statement)
isn't it? (tag).

Negative tags are added to positive statements and positive tags to negative statements.
It's not *cold,* ***is it****?*

The question tag repeats the auxiliary verb or modal auxiliary verb from the statement, and the subject pronoun. If there is no auxiliary verb in the statement, do is used:
You ***like*** *oranges,* ***don't*** *you?*

There are exceptions, for example, imperatives: Sit down, will you?
Please help, won't you?